"Why would someone who 'has it all' chuck it away and walk into an uncertain future? The author does this in dramatic fashion. She walks away from her prestigious law degree, from being a rising star in a large law firm with realistic prospects of fame and fortune. And she quits—just like that. I can relate totally to why she did it. None of the 'rewards' in the path she was on could give her what she really wanted—more joy in life and freedom from the relentless prodding of her 'monkey mind.' If a similar calling is lurking under your skin, you will find her tale entertaining, revelatory, instructive, and well worth reading."

—SRIKUMAR RAO, PhD, The Rao Institute, elite coach, TED speaker, and best-selling author of *Are You Ready to Succeed* and other books

"At some point in everyone's life, a quiet voice inside starts asking, 'Who are you? What are you doing with your life?' In time, that voice becomes louder and more persistent until it forces a journey of self-exploration. As we follow attorney Danielle Sunberg's path in her memoir, *Atlas of Being*, we discover what she was looking for: Direct knowledge that we are far more than our minds and bodies. We are also part of the conscious universe, and we can experience that reality not just as an intellectual exercise, but as vibrantly here and now. *Atlas of Being* is an intimate, emotional, and transformative book. Highly recommended."

—DEAN RADIN, PhD, chief scientist, Institute of Noetic Sciences, and award-winning and best-selling author, *Real Magic* and other books

"Danielle Sunberg has graced us with a remarkable 'travelogue' of consciousness. She shares her personal journey with the pen of a gifted writer and storyteller. Even more importantly, she displays a remarkable depth of authenticity that allows us into her inner world and in doing so allows us to see a path towards our own transformation. It would be hard to read this book without falling in love with this woman and her message. It is a book for anybody, anywhere, at any time in their lives!"

—HOWARD J. ROSS, best-selling author of *Everyday Bias*

"What a gift Danielle Sunberg has given us all in telling her story of one day up-and-quitting her successful lawyer's career to travel the world with her husband in search of The Real, while sharing the deepest of spiritual insights with us and with every chapter ending with questions for further personal reflection on faith, intuition, love, and self-creation of a meaningful life that is always already whole. Danielle's every word rings with an inviting openness and trustworthy intimacy on matters of loss, new life, gratitude, Motherhood, and the poignant re-embracing of her Judaic roots."

—STUART SOVATSKY, PhD, president-emeritus,
Association for Transpersonal Psychology,
author of *Advanced Spiritual Intimacy* and *Words from the Soul*

"A worthwhile and inspiring read for anyone looking to take a leap of faith in life."

—LAURA DAWN, faculty at The Shift Network,
host of The Psychedelic Leadership Podcast, and founder of Grow Medicine

"This is a book to read and to reread. To sit with coffee in hand, looking out into the distance as Danielle has time after time, and to cherish the you that you are, that you have remembered yourself to be, under all the rules, constructs, and boxes that once felt so safe and now feel so untrue. This is one woman's liberation, accessible to all."

—LESLIE TRAUB, principal consultant for Udarta Consulting LLC

"A must read for brave seekers of truth. Danielle's book is packed with insight and will remind you of who you were before the world told you who to be. Each chapter peels away a layer of cultural conditioning until all that's left is raw, naked authenticity.

—MATT MCKIBBIN, co-founder of Decentranet and international speaker

"*Atlas of Being* is a story about authenticity and what it takes to peel off who we think we are to discover who we truly are."
—SUSAN SCHMITT WINCHESTER,
senior vice president & chief HR officer for a fortune 200 company
and co-author of *Healing at Work*, with Martha I. Finney

"Insightful, intimate, and inspiring, Danielle offers us a companion seat on her journey across the globe and through her rising consciousness. With honesty and courage, she invites us to witness her voyage of self-discovery, while gently nudging us to take a look at our own path and offering us encouragement and accessible wisdom along the way."
—MARY OLIVAR, Whole Foods "Healthy Eating Guru," spiritual business mentor, and director for the Center for Shamanic Education and Exchange

ATLAS OF BEING

ATLAS OF BEING

FROM BRIEFCASE TO BACKPACK, ONE FORMER
LAWYER'S EXPLORATION OF THE HUMAN WAY

DANIELLE SUNBERG

For Teddy, Ohm, Minnie, and Sprout,

my soul's travel partners

CONTENTS

FOREWORD

As Danielle illuminates in the deceptively simple *Atlas of Being*, we each have our own path of self-discovery. My path took me to India in my mid-twenties, to the feet of the *guru* (the one who removes the darkness of ignorance) and the practice of *bhakti* (devotional) yoga. Growing up, the concept of a spiritual approach to life had never occurred to me. It took the explosion of consciousness during the mid-to-late Sixties, culturally and chemically induced, to blow my mind and change my perspective.

I have spent many decades now as a substantive editor, helping people give expression to the individual paths they have taken through life. The value of living in the here and now that I learned in the foothills of the Himalayas, Danielle grasped while sipping a latte in Thailand. Sometimes we have to remove ourselves from our comfortable lives to brush off the cobwebs and open a space for the present moment to be revealed to us. Others have had "aha" experiences while stuck in highway traffic during a commute to work or while changing a dirty diaper. As she reminds us, there are no rules for how one becomes aware of the deeper reality that lies beneath our day-to-day lives.

What Danielle is offering in this book is the ancient feminine wisdom that is finally re-emerging in the world—that of embodied grace, of our creative and intuitive abilities to connect with the divine, and what it means to embrace all that we encounter in both the inner and outer realms. This is a wise woman, telling her story. As Michelle Obama said in her book *Becoming*, "There's power in allowing yourself to be known and heard, in owning your unique story, in using your authentic voice."

We need the stories of the women who, like Danielle, are on the inner adventure of awakening—women who have been through the joy of love and the pain of loss. It is through story that we share our laughter and tears with others, that we recognize our common humanity and find our way through the Big Law world, our relationships, and the minutiae of everyday life. Transmission happens, hearts open, spirit is called forth, and new truths reveal that we are not "broken"; we are whole, and wholly ourselves.

Not everyone can whisk off on a trip around the world to discover what lies within. The good news is that it's not necessary. It doesn't matter what you do in the world, what you eat, where you live, or how young or old you are. The Indian saint Sri Ramakrishna had his first inner awakening as a child of six or seven, when he saw a flock of white cranes flying against the dark black rain clouds of the impending monsoon. The astronaut Edgar Mitchell was forty-five when he went to the moon as a "pragmatic test pilot" and returned as a mystic and humanitarian. He said, "On the return trip home, gazing through 240,000 miles of space toward the stars and the planet from which I had come, I suddenly experienced the universe as intelligent, loving, harmonious." Danielle started as a corporate lawyer and now she is a teller of truth, helping others to find their wellness.

If you are longing for more authenticity, for a deeper connection to yourself, others, and the universe, you are already on the path of learning to trust your intuition—the one Dánielle calls *the Voice*—and allowing your heart to lead you to a rich, fulfilling life. In this book, Danielle gifts you with the GPS for navigating the path.

May you follow your own *Voice* to the wonders that await you.

—Parvati Markus

Author of *Whisper in the Heart* (Mandala 2022), *Love Everyone* (HarperOne 2015), and co-author of a children's book, *Isabella Castaspella* (SitaRam Press 2022)

PREFACE

As a young lawyer, I sat at the defendant's table in the federal courthouse day after day, listening to witness examinations and flipping through binders of depositions to confirm matching testimony. I was nothing if not vigilant. Our client was a movie investor facing a six billion dollar claim in a class action lawsuit over the movie's advertisement, and I was going to make sure I lived up to every penny he paid his legal team not to lose his hard-earned fortune.

My life had unfolded along an expected professional path. I pored over my laptop fifteen hours a day, squeezed into pencil skirts, and crammed my feet into high heels. I would have welcomed the pain from pointe shoes, but I begrudged it from my stilettos. I had chosen to be an attorney; it provided financial stability, commanded respect, offered prestige . . . and was utterly devoid of satisfaction.

Each day at my law firm was spent researching, drafting, and filing motions for large, well-funded companies that hired us to help resolve their most challenging problems. The firm's office in downtown Washington D.C., divided into glass fishbowls, kept us associates minute-to-minute accountable to our work. We scurried into the office in the morning and peered down the hall to confirm if we were the first to arrive, as if it were a badge of honor. There was an unstated competition to jockey for the number one position, won by spending the most hours hunched over our desks. We were expected to live and breathe according to the demands of partners, fueled by an incredibly expensive commercial coffee machine right down the hall.

My office was on a long hallway dubbed "Prisoners' Row" that housed five associates. Partners strolled by like prison guards, peering in on us as we clacked away on our keyboards. Handcuffed to our computers, we wanted our jailers to see us working but avoided making eye contact with them, which would have served as an invitation to stop for a chat and inevitably led to us being given more work. Horror stories of vacations cut short, canceled birthday dinners, and receiving the silent treatment from powerful partners created an ominous atmosphere.

I became an anxious person. I never wanted to go to the office and I was afraid to leave at the end of the day. I'd wake up in the morning eyeing the snooze button, not ready to face the steady stream of urgent assignments, the research questions that never had straightforward answers, or the nervous partner-pleasing disposition ("ass-kissing") of my fellow associates. Padding over to my closet, I'd sigh and pick out a power suit to armor myself against another day of cramming in as many billable hours as possible, anathema to my personal motto of efficiency.

During the month-long federal trial defending our movie-investor client, I lived out of a hotel room in St. Louis, Missouri. While I don't make a habit of remembering hotel rooms, I won't forget this one. Those four maroon walls transformed an ordinary box into a spectacular refuge. I'd fling that day's suit jacket over the cream-colored corner chair before flopping into bed at 3 a.m. These precious hours were mine to bathe and sleep before waking up to beat the partners back to the war room in the morning.

Along with the rest of the defense team, every day we alternated back and forth from the courthouse to the "war room," the name bestowed upon the hotel ballroom we reserved for the span of the trial. It was constantly filled with pre-and post-court prep by a team of attorneys, paralegals, assistants, and an endless carousel of food delivery. Riding in on the coattails of extreme sleep deprivation was a nasty cold, and my sneezes shook the courtroom. With a fatigued mind and a worn-down immune system, I had no strength left to swat away *the Voice*.

This Voice wasn't audible to anyone but me. It had been buzzing in my ear for a while now, always pestering me when I had no patience for it. It would continually ask, *"Where are you?"*

It seemed obvious to me. I would hiss "Here!" and swat the Voice away.

Sitting in that courtroom, tired and drained, I heard the Voice ask again, *"Where are you?"*

Too exhausted to fight the Voice, I surrendered. *"I don't know."*

Finally ready to hear whatever this Voice wanted to tell me, it answered the question that had been plaguing me. Quite matter-of-factly, the Voice said, *"You're not here."*

Like an arrow released from the bow, those words shot through my spine. I straightened in my chair and took in the courtroom with fresh eyes. The judge was perched on the bench, listening to the witness being peppered with questions by a gray-haired attorney in an ill-fitting suit. It all seemed to be playing out in slow motion, as if far away on a movie screen.

I had no idea why those words were so powerful, but they shifted something within me and I couldn't shift back.

A few days later, the trial concluded and the legal team flew back home to Washington D.C. to await the jury verdict. We were drained but proud of what we had put in front of the court. As soon as I unlocked the door to my Dupont Circle apartment and rolled in my luggage, already eyeing the bed for a good long nap, my phone rang. It was the lead partner on the case, the salt-and-pepper patriarch of my firm's litigation group. Corner office and all.

"Hello?" I wondered what he had to say.

"Hey, Danielle. I've got great news. The jury came back with a verdict. We won!" He spoke excitedly, but I could hear the exhaustion in his voice.

"Great!" I responded, still eyeing my bed.

"I'm taking a vacation," he continued. "I'll see you back in the office in two weeks."

The office? I hadn't seen my glass fishbowl in a month. My stomach tightened.

My mind raced, and before I could stop myself, I said, "No, actually you won't. I quit."

INTRODUCTION

What had I just done? Of course, I *wanted* to quit. Who doesn't dream about leaving corporate life behind? But I couldn't believe I had done it!

What was I going to do? I feared the unknown, scared of what might come out of my mouth next. But when I thought about never having to go back to that office to cower before the mighty and to be free to live my own life, my body relaxed. My breathing slowed, my confidence rose, and a smile lifted the corners of my mouth. I didn't know the answer to the Voice's question about *where I was*, but I was going to find out.

Who am I? This is the fundamental question of our lives. It rings like a bell, tolling in the distance, louder or softer depending on our phase of life. Like a fractal that shifts through space and time but is always accountable to the same design, we perpetually come back to this root question—*who am I?* No matter what path we take, how many books we read, or how often we stuff the question under the bed, *who am I* reverberates within us.

Wondering *where* I was led me onto a path around the world to try and find myself. The Voice that called to me was the chiming of my inner bell, beckoning me towards what I refer to in this book as inner wisdom, intuition, energy, or natural intelligence. The label is unimportant. What is important is that answering that call offers a glimpse into the truth of who we are.

The truth is, I wrote this book to share the life-changing wisdom that I discovered during my travels so that you don't have to quit your career or wander the globe to get it for yourself. While my path took me to some fairly extreme places, my experiences were merely the envelope in which the "aha" moments were tucked inside. After reading this book, I hope that you open the envelope of your own life experiences. You'll find that revelatory truths can drop in anywhere and at any time.

This book is organized in four parts, each exploring a different dimension of who we are. The wisdom in each section is a patchwork of serendipitous gifts from teachers, friends, colleagues, clients, and my Voice. It is an invitation to dance the tango of life as we explore and redefine the most fundamental aspect of our transformation: *our relationship with ourselves*. Only when we know ourselves, what matters to us, and what we want from life are we truly empowered to take the reins to create our most extraordinary life.

At the end of each chapter is a workbook section with reflections for deeper navigation. They provide the opportunity to integrate your insights and take confident action to transform your life. These sections are easy to skip, as we are prone to saying, "I get it," and moving on. This is your opportunity to slow down and give yourself the space to "get it" at a deeper transformative level. In other words, if you "get it," what are you going to do about it? Use the reflections provided to guide the embodiment of all that comes alive for you.

PART I—MIND, where much of humanity currently lives. We look at thoughts and the true nature of the mind in order to understand how the mind participates in our human operating system. With closer study, we can transform our mind into a friend and trusted partner in life.

PART II—ENERGY, the invisible yet dominant aspect of life that I call my Voice. We dive into what this energy is, how it works, and how to communicate with this guiding force in our lives.

PART III—EXPANSION, understanding the nature of our minds and our energy leads to insights about what we are capable of that expands our notion of who we are. Our relationship to ourselves shifts, which changes how we interact with the world. What is possible in life expands beyond imagining, and problems may completely dissolve.

PART IV—TRANSFORMATION, insights are phenomenal, but the real magic lies in utilizing our insights to create our lives. How do we lead the life we've always dreamed of? How do we create incredible relationships? We are equipped to experience our lives on our own terms and by our own design.

It is likely that you have mastered your life to a certain extent, and yet something deeper calls to you. It's time to dig to this deeper place that you may not have been willing to go before but know you must. It is here that you will discover the enormity of your power. It is this power that is calling you, asking you to create your most satisfying life and your legacy in the world.

I invite you to listen to the chime of your inner bell and discover *your* answer to the question, *"Where are you?"*

PART I

MIND

A being whose awareness is totally free,
who does not cling to anything, is liberated.

—RAM DASS

1

I AM BECOMING

Danielle and Ted in Asheville, North Carolina (2015)

Who we are in this moment does not need to be who we remain, and likely won't. Something strange happens in adulthood where we believe we are done becoming ourselves. In fact, we quite literally become new people every seven years as all the cells in our body are replaced. And so it goes on every level of our being.

I was done being a "D.C. Big Law attorney." It was time to wrap myself in a cocoon, soften my insides, and transform into the next version of myself. Except I had no idea what that would be, which tended to put the kibosh on the whole endeavor. Much of my evolution so far had been unconscious. I was simply "growing up," following the trail of crumbs left by those who came before me.

After that fateful phone call, when I first uttered the words "I quit," I leaned over my bathroom sink and looked in the mirror. I stared into my eyes, something I hadn't done in years, and asked myself two questions, the ripple effects of which I still feel years later: "*Who am I?*" and "*Who do I want to be?*" They catapulted me into a completely different paradigm, defined by a potent combination of self-awareness and empowerment. For the first time, *I* was in control of my next cocoon.

Fear lurked behind this newfound awareness. *If I didn't know what I would look like when I emerged, maybe I shouldn't enter that cocoon at all?* Except I knew that was impossible. Something much more powerful than fear of the unknown was driving me to wrap myself inside these questions—hope, inspiration, liberation, curiosity, and the need to have *my* turn.

It's not that I hadn't changed over the years, but I hadn't been in charge of the process. It's easiest to clock my evolution through my relationship with my husband. Before we started dating, Ted and I became friends as law students in Washington D.C. As he tells it, we met several times before I remembered his name, whereas I was imprinted on his memory from the get-go. I hadn't been husband-shopping, but quite critically, I believed any husband-to-be would *not* be a lawyer.

I very much enjoyed Ted's friendship and we became close, as people who suffer together through law school tend to do. We studied together in a small group of maniacally devoted students, and because we lived only a few blocks from each other, we socialized together on weekends. I'd bring my boyfriend or love interest out to the bar and parade him in front of Ted, seeking his approval. His girlfriend was my friend too, and together we went out to dinner, hiked, and went to trendy social events like an art gallery treasure hunt or Brew at the Zoo, an annual fundraiser where we sipped lagers and peered in on the pandas. In our third year of school, Ted scored some exclusive tickets to Obama's inauguration ball. Since his girlfriend couldn't go with him, I was his platonic date. And it was platonic. There was no undercurrent of romance or flirtation. The very thought of dating him was strange, as if the world would tip over.

4

If you had asked us when we first met who we would turn out to be over the next several years, we would have shrugged our shoulders and muttered, "Employed!" We hadn't given much thought as to who we'd become beyond our careers.

Our friendship gave us incredible access to witness each other grow and transform. At the beginning of law school, Ted flaunted the puffed-up swagger of a recent college fraternity president, which drew some people in and repelled others. It was one of those qualities where one might say, "you have to get to know him," to see past the puffery to the thoughtful, sensitive man underneath.

And that man did deserve his swagger! Blessed with a silver tongue, Ted has always been able to influence people with his quick-witted opinions. It led him to much success, especially as Moot Court champion, law school's souped-up version of debate club. Over time, I watched his machismo soften and transform into the authentic confidence of an admirable leader. He found power in closing his mouth and opening his ears and went from convincing and influencing to connecting and learning.

The obedient young woman Ted met in the school library went through her own transformation. I desperately wanted to master the rules of law . . . and of life. I kept my head down, eyes locked on the tightrope of success as I carefully built my resume, accumulating internships, clerkships, and leadership positions. My life was scheduled for maximum productivity. I almost said no when Ted invited me to the inaugural ball because I had no time in my schedule to go dress shopping! Over the years, Ted watched me turn into a fiery subversive as I learned to raise my gaze and let the world flood in. My rigid way of navigating life melted and morphed until the concept of success became so fluid and formless that it dripped through my fingers.

We watched each other grow and change, peeling off our skins and stepping into new ones. It was only through this change that we grew into the people we wanted to date and marry. (Ted also left the life of a lawyer!) Once in our romantic partnership, our intimate access to each other's evolution allowed us to be the rocks that carved each other's shape.

As my partner, Ted has always been kind and patient with my upsets, tears, and the self-righteous pity I would feel when the world was unfair. He let me be sad and lightly rubbed my back, giving me the comfort I needed by allowing enough validation of however I felt, no matter how ridiculous. He never joined in with my blubbering as my girlfriend might; instead he remained stoic and strong, solid and stable, which I needed to find my way back from grief. Through our relationship and bearing witness to my depth of heart, he became kinder and more patient with his own emotions. He learned to allow his feelings to come up without reflexively stuffing them back down. The toughness of his youth—in which he showed no pain, no fear, and no heartbreak—faded into something gentler. And this transformation, of course, birthed a deeper capacity to sit with the emotional worlds of those he holds dear.

Ted is blessed with feeling safe as he moves through the world. Being in his space is to feel a sense of safety, and I received it from him hungrily and needily. He offers it freely and without trying, as he is simply being Ted. No one can take it away from him, and there is no limit to how much he can give it away. When we dated, he offered this safety to me, which I cherish to this day. I had never experienced unconditional safety in partnership and my body exhaled with a breath I hadn't realized I had been holding. With no need to claw and cling and prove myself, my arms relaxed and reached for new things. Without him, I have no idea if I would have found the courage to leave my legal career behind.

Together we evolved through a choreographed dance from corporate professionals who wore suits and shiny shoes to hippie entrepreneurs who wear sandals and t-shirts. I stopped wearing make-up and straightening my hair. Ted stopped cutting his hair altogether. Over and over again, we went into our cocoons and emerged as someone new.

We got married a month after I quit the law firm. We wrote our own wedding vows as I couldn't imagine reciting an oath to Ted that had not sprung forth from my own heart. The most important lines—the ones that are imprinted on my soul never to fade—are: "I loved who you were the day we started dating. I love who you are today. And I can't wait to love who you will become tomorrow." These words underline the joke that you can have many marriages, all to the same person, reflecting the recognition that we inevitably change. A few days after our wedding, we left our lives in D.C. to become members of the growing tribe of digital nomads who fly across the world on the wings of a backpack and a smartphone.

I had taken the reins over my next cocoon. *"Who am I?"* and *"Who do I want to be?"* wrapped around me, creating the chrysalis that would carry me across six continents to explore what made me not a lawyer, daughter, friend, or wife, but uniquely *me*. *Me* in relationship to myself. Nothing external—not even Ted—would determine who I'd be when I emerged. Not my job, family, finances, or the clothes in my wardrobe would carve my next shape. It was my turn to decide who I was, so I took back the power I had unwittingly bestowed upon the rest of the world.

MILESTONES

Read the *Inner Guidance* bullet points and ask yourself if each one resonates. After you complete the *Deeper Navigation* questions, come back to these bullet points and observe if anything has changed about if and how they resonate. Remember, a one percent change is a change.

INNER GUIDANCE

- We are constantly evolving who we are and how we show up in life, whether or not we realize it.
- We unwittingly bestow the power of our transformation on the rest of the world.
- When we do this, we allow the circumstances and people in our lives to determine how we identify ourselves. Our identities are formed as a response to our relationship with the rest of the world.
- We always have the power to decide who we are, even when it seems like we are at the whim of the world.
- At any and every moment, we can take control of our evolution. When we do this, we build our identity based on our relationship with ourselves.
- This is how we become our true selves.

DEEPER NAVIGATION

1. Think about how you've evolved over your life. Who were you when you were eight? Eighteen? Forty-eight? What has changed and what has stayed the same?

2. Imagine it's ten years in the future. Write yourself a letter describing how you've transformed over these ten years. What's different about you? What's important to you? What's shifted about how you see the world?

3. Pretend you wake up tomorrow in paradise. Describe paradise. What do you do there? Who is with you? How do you feel? Your answers are clues about how you want your life to be.

2

I AM UNDERNEATH

Danielle's office (2016)

On Friday, September 1, 2017, I took the leap. My two weeks' notice was over and it was my last day at my Big Law job, which I spent wandering around the office, bothering colleagues who were not quitting and had mountains of work to do. I confirmed with IT that my laptop would be left on my desk. At 2:30 that afternoon there was a cupcake sendoff, orchestrated by the group-practice leader and attended by various colleagues who were in the office the Friday before Labor Day weekend. Everyone wished me well and the best of luck on my adventure as they selected a cupcake and then promptly returned to work.

I unceremoniously abandoned my office, giving it a quick last sweep for any overlooked personal effects, turned off the light, and took the elevator for the last time. I gave a bland smile to the other person in the elevator, hiding my secret, "You think I work here but I don't. I'm free!"

This leap away from my legal career was layered. In one sense, the leap was geographical. My husband and I packed up our lives and left our home in Washington D.C. to travel the world. Underneath the more obvious leap of journeying the world without a timeline or a destination was the professional layer—a drastic pivot from the legal corporate world to the unknown. While it took courage to let go of financial and professional stability and move forward into uncharted territory, this wasn't the deepest layer. The most powerful and intangible leap was the introspective layer—a leap within to explore my inner "self," a place more exotic and untouched than the farthest corners of the planet.

This is going to get a little "woo," so I'll start with a concrete illustration. I didn't have to pay attention to Ann Taylor sales ever again, something that was almost as automatic for me as checking Instagram anytime I touched my phone. The "Ann Taylor sale" reflex is a byproduct of the ingrained linear professional path. I could unlearn this reflex because, on the surface at least, I had no need to dress for the corporate world anymore.

Let's take this illustration deeper. Being a part of our society is an implicit agreement to believe in particular values. Our identities are then built around these values, and many of us define ourselves in large part by them. This is what we call acculturation, or the process of interweaving who we are with the culture that we live in. One such value is the importance of being successful, a concept defined most often by our careers. Most of us have professional goals. I'm not saying professional goals should be abandoned on the journey of self-discovery, but it is important to recognize these occupational achievements as our society's currency for self-worth. It's a constructed concept capitalized on by clothing retailers who play to our egos by marketing suits and ties with the promise of feeling powerful at work and thereby validating our worth. Thus, the closet full of Ann Taylor.

Of course, I could find success outside of my career, but it had never occurred to me to look. Maharishi Mahesh Yogi, the father of

Transcendental Meditation (TM), one of my meditation disciplines, wisely said, "Being happy is of utmost importance. Success in anything is through happiness." I embraced this quote, in which success remains undefined, unconstrained, and certainly unrelated to showing off a corner office or a bank account. Happiness for Maharishi is not the stroke of the ego. Otherwise, I would have finished the journey exactly where I started—needing to prove my self-worth in a big shiny fishbowl wearing an Ann Taylor suit.

So, my leap wasn't only the choice to explore the world or a pivot away from corporate life. It was also a space I opened up for introspection—to explore who I was without being tied to an identity founded on societal constructs of who I *should* be. The "Washington D.C Big Law attorney" persona I had been perfecting over the years was no longer how I wanted to show up in the world.

I had no idea who I was underneath my Ann Taylor suit. I spent most of my last two weeks at the office thinking wildly about who I would be once I didn't work there anymore. I constructed endless stories and identities about who I was—a tall woman with long brown hair, a liberal Jew from New York, an athlete with too many gym shoes, an overeducated unemployed millennial statistic. I was up to my eyeballs in stories about myself, but none of them captured what I imagined was my essence.

Research indicates we have thousands of thoughts a day, and likely thousands more subconscious thoughts that can't yet be measured or quantified. We are swimming in a pool of thoughts from the time we wake up to when we fall asleep at night, and we ascribe much value and importance to these lingual rockets that constantly blast through the space inside our heads. Because our society so highly values the skills of the mind, we've come to spend most of our time and attention focused here. As a civilization, we spend incredible amounts of money educating the mind, training it to reach its highest potential for capitalization. I don't remember most of the content I learned in college, but it doesn't matter. I learned something vastly more important from my liberal arts education—*how to think*. This was the real prize, as mastering the art of reason and logic allows us to synthesize complex concepts and ideas better than any computer.

We should indeed value this exquisite tool of the mind. You're probably sitting on a comfortable chair right now, thanks to the power of our minds.

Some caveman got sick of having a sore tush and thought there had to be a better way to sit and rest. After trying with sticks and rocks and logs, *voila*, the first rudimentary chair. One day not too long ago, humans decided to explore outer space. Of course, that was only possible with the mind's participation. It was envisioned, planned, and executed with the help of the mind. Our minds work brilliantly to solve the world's most complex puzzles, innovate never-before-seen solutions, and invent new technologies that vastly improve our lives.

However, *living* in my mind meant that instead of being in control of my thoughts, my thoughts controlled me. Any time I peeled off a story of who I was, another was there waiting for me. I rode an elevator up and down a tall tower, each floor a different story defining who I was. While I could get off at any story I wanted, I could not seem to leave the building; I was forever trapped by my thoughts about myself, with no story any truer than any other. After going up and down and up and down, I gave up trying to think my way to who I truly was.

If there was a "me" underneath all my thoughts, I needed a different guide to find her. I looked to my Voice to show me the exit sign out of the building. I had no idea where I was going, but I felt a deep trust that heeding my Voice's call would take me where I needed to go. I *knew*, beyond logic or reason, that this inner Voice would take me to myself— the Danielle who was solid, constant, and while silently present on each floor of the building, she existed just as well outside its walls. I can't explain with logic or reason how I knew this. There was no synthesis of data or rationale to work out, but my whole body sang in tune with this Voice. I followed its call to fly halfway around the world and hoped I'd find what I was looking for.

MILESTONES

INNER GUIDANCE

⌇ We spend years perfecting our personas. Once we decide on our identity, we show up in the world that way.

⌇ These personas are mental constructs created by the incredible tool of the mind.

⌇ We have come to identify so closely with our personas, we forget that they are only constructs. They are no more the truth of who we are than a sweater we wear.

⌇ Exploring who we are underneath our constructs is one of the most empowering adventures of our lives. It is a journey we can take anywhere in the world and with anyone we want, but ultimately the process of self-discovery is a solo trek that navigates us in one direction—inside ourselves.

⌇ This exploration allows us to play with identities the same way we play with our wardrobe. This is when the fun begins.

DEEPER NAVIGATION

1. How would you describe yourself? List all the labels that you would apply to the persona you've been perfecting over your lifetime.
2. Which labels do you enjoy wearing, and why? Notice how you feel as you embody each label.
3. If you could wave a magic wand and remove all your labels, who would you be? It's okay if you don't know the answer. This is a chance to envision many possibilities that make you smile.

3

I AM PRESENCE

Danielle and Ted at temple Wat Phra That Doi Suthep in Thailand (2017)

On October 26, 2017, five days after marrying my husband, two months after leaving my law firm, and after seven years of living in Washington D.C., Ted and I packed up our Dupont Circle apartment and moved it into storage. We were about to embark on an open-ended voyage, traveling the world for as long as we felt inspired to be dandelion seeds blowing in the wind.

We took pains scrutinizing the furniture, art, and odds and ends, trying to decide what our future selves would want in our hypothetical future house after we finished our travels and would need chairs to sit on and pots and pans to cook with. The rest we gifted to friends and family, thrusting cookware and end tables at them, hoping to convince them that they needed an entire set of picture frames or that they should also take the lamp because it really complemented the blender.

We said goodbye to the lives we had built in Washington D.C., slipped our backpacks over our shoulders, and drove to Dulles airport to board a plane with one-way tickets in hand. The next chapter of our lives was waiting. I wondered if it was where *I* was waiting.

After a stop in Doha, Qatar, and a proper honeymoon at a beautiful Thai resort, we settled into an apartment in the Nimman neighborhood of Chiang Mai, the biggest city in northern Thailand whose exoticness hooked me immediately. Southeast Asia bore little resemblance to the world I knew. It was foreign in language, culture, religion, values, food, sense of humor, fashion, and politics. The Thai interpret life differently than Americans, and the pillars of the community were certainly not the resume values that built the foundation of Washington D.C. It didn't matter what these pillars were; it was their difference that was intoxicating.

Experiencing the world in this vacuum where I knew nothing and could judge nothing was both liberating and uncomfortable. I didn't know the rules, norms, or customs. The right way to do things in the States wasn't necessarily now wrong, it simply wasn't relevant. This is exactly what I was looking for in the home that would cradle the birth of my true self and so I accepted the discomfort as the price of carte blanche. I looked forward to turning the labels that defined me inside out and discarding them so that I could be born anew.

Initially I was quite intimidated, as is often the case when we have no idea what is going on around us. The last thing I wanted to do was accidentally offend anyone or appear foolish. Motorbikes zipped between cars on congested roads that offered only the rare pedestrian crosswalk, so I couldn't even cross the street without playing a deadly arcade game of Frogger. The fear and anxiety at doing something so simple exposed my foreignness. Meanwhile, the locals floated across the street with their eyes closed.

I constantly wondered, "*How do I...*" and "*Is it okay to...*" Was it polite to take home leftovers from restaurants? Could I say hello to the monks who populated the city? Should I bow to them or was that a Western misappropriation of their tradition and religion? What did people eat for breakfast? How did I say thank you? I felt the friction of the unknown in everything I did, in every interaction. Dealing with the unknown can be exhausting. It's why we sigh with relief when we see McDonalds or Starbucks in another country—it's the same everywhere and we know the answers to "How do I?" and "Is it okay to?"

Eventually I figured it out. With hand gestures and smiles, I ordered chicken from our neighborhood street vendor and asked for only a little sweetened coconut milk in my morning coffee. I learned how to walk the city without facing down death at every intersection. Friction eased and interactions became smoother. Not because I learned all the customs or how to speak Thai, but my fear and apprehension in approaching people and making a fool of myself subsided. I got over myself. Pointing at things and smiling became easier than mentally freaking out about not knowing what to say. I remembered my true mother tongue and gave voice to the true universal language of kindness.

But the questions I intended to ask myself seemed to have gotten shoved down to the bottom of my backpack and forgotten about, replaced with the more urgent priority of learning how to live there. It was about halfway through our stay in Chiang Mai that I even remembered that I was supposed to be exploring these questions. *Who am I? Where am I?* I felt the head-smacking shame that I had gotten myself all the way to Thailand and promptly forgotten what I had traveled there to do! Okay, fine. I had remembered the value of kindness and learned how to cross the street, but did that add up to anything meaningful?

After a few days of self-flagellation, I gave myself a reprieve. I psyched myself up, "Danielle, your time here isn't over. It's only begun. Of course, you needed time to adjust. Now you can turn your focus to finding answers to the questions you've come here to explore."

I liberated myself from guilt, but the pressure was on. It was like I had given myself permission to acclimate to the altitude, and now that I could breathe, I had to climb the mountain. If I didn't make it to the top, what kind of guilt would find me then? What if I traveled around the world and never summited? After a day or two of suffering this proactive anxiety that afflicts us overachievers, I noticed it. I pointed my finger at the anxiety hovering over my shoulder and commanded, "You there! Stop!"

Smirking back at me, my anxiety said, "You caught me. Here I am driving you nuts, but what are you going to do about it?"

Good question. Touché, anxiety.

I thought about it as I walked past the jackfruit trees and the sprinkle of motorbikes that lined the street on the way to my favorite coffee shop. The baristas were award-winning latte artists, and every time I ordered a coffee I sipped a delicious surprise in the form of an animal, dragon, tree, or symbol woven into the frothed milk. Sitting under the umbrella shade with my coffee, I let my mind wander.

What was the best way to start my quest? I would create a plan. I would scour the city for new experiences and give myself the goals of interacting with at least three new people, journaling, and meditating every day. I could create some kind of "how to find out who you are" manual for myself. But honestly, that sounded exhausting! I was enjoying doing what I wanted to do when I wanted to do it, or not doing anything at all, a freedom that had eluded me for years. I wasn't really interested in giving that up. Quite the opposite. I wanted to integrate this fluidity more deeply in my life.

Then I thought, "What if I created a plan and executed it and it didn't work?" How much more guilt could I pile on myself if I committed to a plan that I had no confidence in *and* didn't achieve the results? Yikes.

I went back to basics. What did I know for sure? What I knew was that this journey was intended to be fun, a critical ingredient missing from my former life. If creating a plan didn't sound like fun, then I wouldn't do it. Simple as that. That was all I knew, and it was all I needed to save me from throwing myself full throttle in an unfun, stressful direction.

"But what is the *right* direction?" I wondered.

I closed my eyes and breathed in the aroma of my coffee. Its nutty scent curled into my nostrils. The beans came from up the road, grown and harvested in the national preserves north of Chiang Mai. As I breathed in the earthy roast, I listened to the unintelligible chatter of groups of Thai friends sitting at nearby tables. The staccato melodies of their conversation were punctuated with bursts of laughter. The heat of the sun moved across the sky, edging over the umbrella and warming my legs. My senses filled to the brim as time sailed by. Something hooked my ribs and caught my breath, pulling me out of the moment and back to my thoughts, but it was too ethereal and slipped through the space in my bones.

What was that? Something important. I opened my eyes. It felt so close and yet so far away. *An answer to something.* The more I tried to think about it, the less I could grasp it. I rolled my head around on my neck, shook it off, and asked myself what had triggered this slippery knowing?

"I don't know," I thought.

I waited.

Nothing. I gave up.

"*Something,*" I insisted, curling my hands into fists on the table.

I sat there waiting, committed to patience. I closed my eyes again. And then, like a bolt of lightning it struck me: *I let it all go.* I had let go of the questions, let go of the search. I let go of why I was sitting in this chair, why I had quit my job, why I was in Thailand altogether. I was simply in the moment. The power of it came effortlessly, almost sneakily. Where did that come from? And why did that feel so important? My mind worked furiously to pinpoint an answer. The deeper I furrowed my brows in thought, the further out of reach the answers seemed to be. I couldn't pin down what I didn't know, and the elusiveness of the answers I craved stressed me out.

After failing to mentally squeeze out the unknowable, I surrendered the gig. When I let go of the hunt for what I didn't know and let it fade into the background, what I did know came rushing to the surface. Suddenly, I saw everything I *do* know, and that is a treasure trove. I hadn't given myself any credit for what I knew because I was always on the hunt to know *more*. All this wisdom had been sitting there patiently the whole time, only I was too hurried chasing other answers to see it.

There is a magic in untangling ourselves from the chase *to know more*. The alchemy of *slowing down* is the space it creates to notice thoughts we typically zoom past—solutions, creativity, inspiration, and insights. Indeed, our "aha" moments often come when we are in the shower because we have simply slowed down. Pop! In comes our genius. Underneath our thinking mind, we are full of calm clarity, at least until our thoughts catch our attention and pull us away.

Years later my coach and mentor, Jennie, gave me the following analogy to explain this experience. Imagine that you are a transparent water bottle about half-filled. The water represents your mind in its natural calm and clear state. How lovely! Then pour sand into your bottle, with each grain of sand representing a thought. Being caught in thought loops—thinking about something repeatedly that you can't let go of—is like shaking the bottle, mixing the sand and water into a murky brown liquid, making it impossible to see anything clearly.

How do you get the water in the bottle to clear? The nature of sand is that it will settle to the bottom if left alone and the water will naturally rise to the top. You regain your natural state of calm and clarity. In this natural state, we have space to see new and different thoughts. The effortless way to detach from our thought loops is simply to notice that all we are doing is shaking our bottle . . . and all we have to do is set it down. In other words, *do nothing*.

When I stopped chasing the answers, I set down my water bottle. In doing nothing, in popped my wisdom. *Nothing* caused the power of that moment. It wasn't the enjoyment of a good meal, a funny movie, or a crazy exotic Thai experience that connected me to the vibrancy of life. I was having a cup of coffee, something I've done so many hundreds of times that I barely noticed it anymore. But this time I noticed it. I was fully immersed in the experience. I remembered why I did this small thing of sipping from a hot mug in the warm sun. I loved it.

After basking in this remembrance for a few moments I asked myself, "*What do I do with this?*" And this is where sitting without knowing, letting go of chasing the answer, surrendering the whole damn puzzle offered me the most immediate and clear answer. What I knew to be true from that moment of *nothing* was that I felt more connected to my life than I had in a very, very long time. I felt free, in flow, unburdened, vibrant.

Here I am. I told the Voice. I am *here*, tucked inside the experience.

I was in the experience of *every* moment, and all I needed to do was be there to witness it. Gleefully, I let go of the reflex to draft up a full plan and leaned into the confidence that swelled in my chest. This wisdom offered one simple piece of guidance to follow: *be present.* Be an observant participant in life, without judgment. This was something I could give myself without pressure or anxiety. It lit me up inside and the smile on my face began to hurt. I put together my two pieces of wisdom: *have fun* and *be present.* They directed me to *Enjoy the Moment.* This "plan" required nothing of me. I didn't need to talk to three people a day or go somewhere new or try something I didn't want to do. It allowed me to do what I wanted, when I wanted, as long as I was in the moment. I already knew it would work because I had just experienced it.

The shackles of needing a goal, something that had been an integral part of my life, slipped off my wrists. I couldn't see the whole path forward, but one step was enough: *enjoy the moment.* One step is always enough, as it is only as much as I can address at one time. The rest of the plan I thought I needed lived in the realm of the mind, always searching to know more. This realm is hypothetical as it assumes there will be no curve balls or serendipitous moments that might change the landscape of my path entirely. A "complete" plan might have offered my mind psychological safety, but no actual control.

Newly invigorated, I floated through Chiang Mai, fully experiencing the city through all my senses. I embraced my Western habits even though they stuck out hideously and reminded myself to experience what it is like to stick out without judging myself. I embraced Thai customs that I had picked up, telling myself to experience what it was like to assimilate them without judgment.

I experienced moments large and small as I climbed temple steps and listened to the slap of my sandals against the slick, worn stones. A moment sliding into the red bench at my local noodle shop and ordering a Pad Thai. A moment receiving a Thai massage and feeling the pain of being stretched and twisted by bony supple hands. A moment of being sick of Thai food and crossing town with Ted to grab chicken schnitzel for dinner at a popular Israeli restaurant. These moments flashed one after the other. I remembered each experience—feeling it again, tasting it again, hearing it again. The moments, each their own picture, connected to form a larger mosaic. As I zoomed out to see the full collage, I understood something deeply: *I was having a love affair with life.* All I had done was to make sure I was present to witness it.

MILESTONES

INNER GUIDANCE

- ⤷ We have been trained to use our rational minds to navigate life. When we don't know what to do, our minds do their best to seek answers. These answers tend to be external—from an article, a friend, or collected data.
- ⤷ When we can't find an answer, we might feel stressed, confused, and overwhelmed.
- ⤷ When we feel stressed, confused, or overwhelmed, we tend to work harder to find an answer in hopes those feelings will disappear.
- ⤷ When we stop chasing the answers we don't have and listen for the answers already within us, we find a deep well of wisdom—and serenity.
- ⤷ One way to access the answers within us is by slowing down and being present in the moment (in other words, *do nothing*). When our minds slow down, we are able to notice other thoughts—our creativity, inspiration, and insights.
- ⤷ This process is universal, meaning it works regardless of context or content. It doesn't matter what answer we are looking for. It applies to everyone, for every thought.

DEEPER NAVIGATION

1. Reflect over your life to a time when you experienced insights, big or small. Notice where you were and what you were doing, what your headspace was, and see if you can remember the feeling. An insight can simply be a small "aha" moment, or it can be as huge as, "How did I not see that before!" Relax into this. The more you chase down insights, the less available they may be.
2. Tune into how your insights tend to drop in for you. Are they feelings, thoughts, a body sensation, a visual, a sound, or something else?
3. What do you usually do when you don't know something? When does clarity seem to drop in? List all the things you usually do when you are seeking clarity. What works best, and why?

4

I AM AWARE

Danielle speaking with a monk Wat Phra That Doi Suthep in Thailand (2017)

As the weeks in Thailand rolled by, my behavior changed. I spoke less often, filling the air with less idle chatter. I listened more. I listened to my surroundings, the soundtrack of my life. I listened to the language I didn't understand buzzing all around me, to the birds chattering in the mango trees, to the temple prayers, to the honks of motorbikes swerving through traffic, to the sizzle of meat grilling on street corners. I couldn't understand anything, so I couldn't judge anything. I didn't know the customs and I couldn't decipher the rightness or wrongness of social interactions, so I simply watched and listened.

Quiet presence allowed for a deeper awareness of my thoughts. I began to notice my own reactions to life. I had become a witness to myself. I noticed I was annoyed that the symbols intended to differentiate the shampoo from the conditioner bottle in no way did so, or oddly delighted that the Italian food I ordered to be delivered to the apartment came in clear, plastic sandwich bags, both the soup and the lasagna. I had no context for the way life worked in Thailand, so I unconsciously brought forth my well of life-experience from a different corner of the globe. What became clear was the futility of applying any formerly acceptable expectations to this new place. Everything was different here, and it was much easier to allow it to be the way it was.

"Okay," I thought, scooping bagged lasagna onto a plate. "What do I do with my perspective? Throw it away? Is it useless?" Even if I had wanted to throw it away wholesale, it seemed to insert itself without my asking.

The next evening Ted and I ate at a neighborhood restaurant called Cherng Doi that specialized in crispy grilled chicken that we dipped in a delicious sauce alongside sticky rice and papaya salad. After a fabulous meal stuffing ourselves, the waiter seemed to ignore us. He never brought the check, no matter how hard we tried to lock eyes and make the universal waving motion for "check please." I thought, "How rude," and then caught myself. I was frustrated. For fifteen minutes, I had been sitting there politely trying to catch the waiter's attention and feeling completely ignored. I was projecting an expectation based on my previous experiences about how to ask for the check onto this poor kid and getting mad at him for not meeting it.

Finally, I walked up to the hostess and pointed at my credit card, shrugged, and mouthed, "Check?" She nodded and pointed to the small green plastic cards placed on each of the wooden picnic tables with numbers on them. Apparently, at this restaurant you paid at the hostess stand by giving her your table number and she pulled the associated check. Well, expectations be damned! I realized I had the choice to feel frustrated by an expectation that the waiter had never agreed to meet or I could let it go.

I thought more about how often my thoughts, my mood, and my reactions were controlled by unmet expectations that I didn't realize I was projecting onto the world around me. When I thought I was being ignored by the waiter, I felt annoyed and even wondered if I was being slighted as a westerner. I had no reason to think that, but *I needed to reconcile his behavior with my expectations*. I hadn't even realized I was doing it. Electricity sparked as it dawned on me what it meant to be run by the unconscious mind, and I felt sick in my stomach that I was letting it run me. New questions emerged: *Had I been doing this my whole life? What does this mean about who I am? How do I untangle myself from this reflexive way of responding to life?*

To answer these questions, I called upon what I had learned weeks earlier at the coffee shop: *slow down*. Rather than push for answers right there and then, I let them flow in on their own time. This relaxed pace of patiently waiting was the opposite of my former life in Washington D.C., where every question was urgent and I'd better hustle for the answer. Sleeping on it was a last resort, not a cozy invitation.

What came through over the next week was a dissertation on how I generated my experience of life. My inner wisdom appeared during my walks to the supermarket, as I sipped Thai iced tea and daydreamed at the laundromat, and when I rested under the shade of one of Chiang Mai's hundreds of temples. How I had created my life up until that moment may not have been what I would have chosen had I known what I was doing, but now I saw how it worked and that dropped me right into the driver's seat of my life. I had been pointing my finger out at the world around me, accusing people and situations of causing me distress, anger, and all the rest. What I saw so clearly for the first time was that my life was playing out according to *my thoughts*. I had reacted to how my expectations played out at the restaurant, not the scene itself.

I noticed how slick and seamless this process of consciousness is. How quickly I could think a thought, project it outward on the movie screen of my life, and then experience it. It was instantaneous. Most of the time I had no idea that I was making a movie of my very own, acting in it, and watching it at the same time. It didn't matter how justified I felt pointing my finger at the waiter, the president, or my broken washing machine. It was always my own thoughts that I was experiencing.

Thoughts are the ultimate creative force. Previously I hadn't given my thoughts much credit; they were these intangible flies buzzing around in my head. Now I understood that my thoughts generated my entire experience. As creative forces, thoughts have incredible power, which is why we are admonished as children that if we have nothing nice to say, it's best not to say anything at all. One word can cut someone to the core, build someone up, or calm someone down. I often found myself at the whim of words—both those I said to myself and those that others said to me.

Understanding the power of thought shifted me into the role of scriptwriter, and it was up to me whether I wrote a comedy or a tragedy. I could live in a world where I was beholden to my expectations or a world where I offered grace to everyone in it, including myself. At the chicken restaurant, I reflexively projected my expectations about what I thought ought to happen onto my waiter and the only person it caused distress to was me.

This insight about how I created my life with my thoughts was one of those deeply personal yet universal "aha" moments, like a landscape forever changed by a bolt of lightning. We all have thoughts—our thinking mind is a gift bestowed upon humanity—and we are in the unique position to be aware of our thoughts. If our thoughts are the playdough we use to generate our experience, it's up to us how we squish words and mold our thoughts to create and destroy reality. At the chicken restaurant I had molded my playdough into a shape that was delicious, exotic, and frustrating. The shape of my playdough wasn't *wrong*, but it wasn't objectively true. It didn't apply to everyone, and I couldn't imagine what anyone else's perspective was. I have no idea what shape Ted made with his playdough, or the waiter, or the Thai family sitting one table over from us.

The word *subjective* bloomed like a lily freshly watered. There are eight billion perspectives on the planet, each engineered with a unique blend of ideas, expectations, desires, and fears. It's one thing to recognize that people have their own opinions about art, politics, and religion, and another to extend this recognition to every crack and crevice of life. Absolutely no one else hears music the way you do, brushes their teeth the way you do, or loves their mother the way you do. My new understanding of subjectivity set me free from servitude to my perspective. I was liberated from rigid devotion, demanding that everyone else see through my eyes and call it *the way it is*. It was only *one* perspective, and there was nothing that made it more right or wrong, good or bad than any other perspective.

While I would no longer foist my perspective on anyone else, there is another side of the coin. My perspective, but one of eight billion, is *mine*. Of course, I am invested in *my* experience of life. While there is much power in loosening the grip on my perspective, my perspective is my power. *My* thoughts give my life meaning. Not Ted's, not my mother's, not my neighbor's. *Mine.* I am blessed to be one of eight billion perspectives in the world, and mine is entitled to be experienced in the same way that my heart is to beat. *My* perspective imbues meaning onto life itself, and that is extraordinary.

My playdough squished and stretched as my perspective expanded to embrace this new understanding. I changed. I cared less to convince Ted or anyone else about anything. No one needed to co-sign my perspective and I didn't need to sign onto theirs. Being understood has always been deeply important to me. It's likely why I became so infatuated with language and enjoyed being a lawyer—a deep obsession with choosing the exact right word to convey the exact right meaning. There's a reason there are synonyms! The slight nuance in words holds all the power in being understood. In the legal profession, we tend to conflate being understood with agreement; if you understand me, you'll agree with me. We tend to do this in life, too. If Ted could understand where I was coming from, could crawl inside my mind and see life through my perspective, then he would understand and agree with what I said and what I did.

Paying the check that night allowed me to disentangle the two. I can still convey myself as accurately as I know how, but whether anyone agrees with my perspective isn't up to me. In a beautiful way, I was glad to give up the fight, to release the tension I had been holding onto for decades in which my perspective needed validation. I was glad to let other people have theirs, and I was glad to be entitled to mine.

I've noticed a very captivating path in which people yearn for a singular truth. It's critical that they know *the way it is*. Some use their minds like a vacuum to consume all information in an effort to form a "correct" perspective of the world. Others perform a sort of emptying out, weeding out all meaning from their experience in hopes of never forming a perspective in the first place. If whatever perspective we see life through is like a pair of tinted sunglasses that add a blue or pink hue to reality, some people endeavor to remove those glasses entirely and see the world for how it "truly" looks. Whichever direction is chosen is the same journey down the path of absolute, static, *objective* truth. If it is human nature to think, and it is our thinking that makes us unique, why do so many feel compelled to peel off their humanity? Why do so many yearn for instructions in molding their playdough, or wish to throw it out the window?

The real privilege in becoming aware of the power of my thoughts was in embracing the magic of both sides of the coin. Holding two seemingly incompatible ideas at the same time is an incredible human ability. We each have a perspective that can only ever be ours, a mere speck on the planet of eight billion realities. None more true than anyone else's. At the same time, each perspective is sacred because it is *our* truth, used to create *our* life. We are the masters of our reality, so keep playing with your playdough.

MILESTONES

INNER GUIDANCE

- We tend to believe that our experience of life is shaped from the outside in. This is a misunderstanding of the way our minds work.
- Thoughts are creative forces that generate our experience of life from the inside out. Our thoughts determine how we feel and respond to life.
- Our experience of life is subjective. The way we think and feel about an experience is uniquely ours.
- Our perspective of life is critical to our humanity as it gives our life meaning.
- Our perspective of life does not need to be right to be sacred.

DEEPER NAVIGATION

1. Explore listening to yourself or to someone else without an agenda or expectation. There is no need to listen for anything in particular or to respond. You don't need permission to do this. See if this simple act shifts how you participate in the conversation and understand the other person. Does it change how the other person behaves?

2. Notice when you point your finger at someone else or at a situation as responsible for your actions and your mood. What was your headspace at the time? Look at how your thoughts were the source for how you felt and acted.

3. Over the next week, recognize that regardless of what you say and do, you are doing the best you can in the moment. You are experiencing your thinking, which informs what your best looks like.

4. Notice how as your level of understanding yourself increases, so does your awareness of others. When you are interacting with others, notice that they are also experiencing their thinking. When you remember that they are also doing the best they can in the moment, what shifts for you? Does how you show up in the relationship change?

5

I AM BELIEF

Danielle and friends on a sailing trip in Greece (2018)

The power of thoughts rattled around in my head as we trekked west from Asia to Europe. I wanted to dig in deeper and understand this ultimate creative force. What made thoughts so powerful?

The summer unfolded for us on the Aegean. We skipped along the Greek islands, spending a few weeks on different idyllic shores, waking up to the sparkling sea and hopping on a scooter to explore every bakery and taste all the baklava we could get our hands on before sitting down at a café to get in a few hours of work. I joined Ted's technology startup to cut my teeth in the entrepreneurial world. We'd watch the sun sink into the sea as we drank white wine and ate grilled fish drizzled with local fresh-pressed olive oil. Each meal started with a bowl of olives and ended with a shot glass filled with sweet Greek yogurt and fruit. I'd spend afternoons sitting on our balcony watching little boats sail in and out and sketching the trees that framed the marina.

Hopping from tiny island to tinier island, we trundled off to a fishing town called Piso Livadi on the edge of Paros, the hidden gem of the Cyclades. Our three-story house featured a spiral staircase running up the middle; it overlooked the water on one side and backed to an alley shared with restaurants on the other. The warm doughy smell of fresh-baked bread wafted into our house each morning. Every few days the family we rented the house from swung by with freshly made ouzo and fruit jams. Life was bliss.

Weeks rolled by like the waves. There was nothing to plan except which beach to sprawl out on for the afternoon. Presence showed up in Greece with ease, lazily offering itself as the only option. There was no worrying to distract me from my sandcastles. After three weeks on Paros and then a month on the bustling port island of Syros, we joined three couples for a week-long boat trip sailing around the small islands close to the mainland. We piled all our luggage onto a 42-foot catamaran and met our sea captain. Steve was an ex-pat Brit fueled by cigarettes and light beer, with a secret agenda to sail wherever he wanted despite our requests. We never saw him eat a full meal or drink any water, but he was competent and kind, and he navigated us everywhere safely.

On the fifth day of our nautical adventure, we asked Steve to take us to a remote uninhabited island he had told us about, a golf course-sized wrinkle of sand with an inlet offering room for one boat. We'd have the island to ourselves and, according to Steve, it was known for dolphin spotting. We were thrilled at the idea. We plotted our course and sailed off, expecting the voyage to take a little over an hour. Reclining on the boat deck we talked and laughed, smelling of coconut and sweat. Steve called for our attention after about twenty minutes and pointed to dark clouds in the distance.

"There's a storm coming," he shouted over our music, making a megaphone by cupping hands over his mouth. We looked at him nervously.

"Don't worry," he waved us off. "We'll beat the storm and ride it out on the island. We'll be protected by the cove. By the time you're finished eating lunch, it'll be sunshine and dolphins."

We gave him a thumbs up and turned up the volume on our music. Another twenty minutes went by and the clouds loomed closer. As the island came into view, so did a yacht that was already docked there.

"Bad news," Steve reported after pulling up to the boat and speaking to the crew. "The inlet doesn't have space for two boats and that yacht isn't leaving until tomorrow. We are going to have to find somewhere else to ride out the storm."

My friend Amalie, a woman with bright blonde hair and an easy laugh, spoke up. Voice quivering, she asked Steve, "Where are we going to go?" She had been wearing a seasickness patch behind her ear for the last five days and was not looking forward to being tossed around in big waves.

"Well, I don't think there's another island around here," Steve put his hand over his eyes to block the sun and surveyed his map. "I don't see anywhere we can get to before the storm starts," he said as he took a drag on his cigarette.

I glanced over at Amalie. She grabbed her boyfriend's hand and tried to look brave. Steve shrugged and took a swig of beer. "Our best bet is to sail away from the storm. We'll catch a bit of it, but it won't be bad as long as we are in open water. No boats to crash into." He smiled and let out the sail to swing us around, heading away from our little oasis and the promise of dolphins.

The wind started to pick up and the dark clouds threatened to obscure the glow of the sun. Amalie looked like a hostage, trapped and scared, and she scooted closer to her boyfriend Wyatt. Together they watched our giant unicorn floaty that was strapped to the back of the boat as it violently bobbed up and down like a bucking bronco. Our other friends parked themselves somewhere dry and buckled down for the storm, not quite white-knuckling their seats, but not about to dance to the music still blasting on the speakers. Meanwhile, Ted and I ran inside and whipped through our bags, digging around until we found our rain jackets. Tucking them under our arms we burst out onto the boat deck, ready to rock and roll in the waves. Ted ran up to the bow and turned his face into the rain that streamed down in fat drops. Not quite as daring, I held onto the side of the boat where I could still hear the music and did a little rain dance.

Steve was now under his rain hood, the tip of his cigarette peeking out. His beer was safely stowed in a cup holder as huge waves rolled under the boat, rocking us side to side. The sky turned completely grey and dripped into the sea, swallowing it except for the white froth on the tips of the waves that sneered at us, threatening to come aboard and pull us in. I glanced over at Amalie, who was huddled with Wyatt, praying to live through the storm.

"Alright, you two," Steve beckoned to Ted and me. I thought he was going to tell us to sit down. "You really ought to have shoes on, and Ted, come over to the side where Danielle is." We nodded obediently and howled arm-in-arm into the storm. The fact that Steve instituted some type of limitation led me to believe he was indeed paying attention, which inspired my bravery to continue dancing as it was apparently within the limits of safe storm sailing. Now completely soaked, we had no use for the rain jackets and shed them to merge as one with the weather.

"Aren't you guys scared?" Amalie called to us.

"I'm from Florida!" Ted answered. He grew up on boats and hurricanes were a season like fall or winter.

I thought Ted's answer, while honest, wasn't helpful to Amalie, who seemed to be grasping for a reason to let go of some of her fear. "Steve doesn't seem concerned," I offered, although taking cues from Captain Steve wasn't really something I recommended in most other situations. "We can all swim and the sea is warm," I added, hoping I'd thrown out a few straws for Amalie.

"Oh god," Amalie covered her face with her hands. She was trapped on a boat with lunatics. Wyatt chuckled and gave me a thumbs up, but he looked quite content to stay dry under the deck roof.

After a while, Steve told us he was heading towards an island he'd been to once before, and we'd arrive in about fifteen minutes. The grey horizon gave no indication that such an island existed, but Amalie, who was looking a little green, perked up considerably. Our other friends nodded seriously, like they had received a medical prognosis that they were going to live, but only if they continued to sit stoically for the remainder of the storm. I looked around for Ted and found him standing on the second level of the catamaran chatting with Steve as rain pummeled his face. *He would make a good pirate*, I thought. I went inside the boat to grab a towel and dry off, holding onto kitchen cabinets and countertops to keep from falling over.

"You alright?" I asked as I plopped down next to Amalie, a little harder than expected as we got slapped by a wave. She was hunched over her phone, busy texting notes of love and farewell to her family and friends.

"You and Ted are nuts," she said as she looked up at me. "You could have fallen off the boat and died. Or slipped and really hurt yourself."

I shrugged as I squeezed out my hair. She was right, but fear didn't come to me in the form of mortality. It came dressed in the cloak of failure, hovering over my shoulder whispering words of self-doubt.

"Look, the island!" I saw the beach poking through the clouds. We were close, maybe two or three minutes away.

We pulled into a little cove protected by a hill and completely absent of other boats. Someone needed to jump into the water to tie us up and Wyatt volunteered—a chance to shake off fear and be a hero. The rain had already calmed down quite a bit and we could see the craggy trees that dotted the shore. Wyatt splashed in the shallow water with the rope and swam the few feet over to the beach. He climbed a branch of a tree leaning over in the wind and knotted the rope around it.

"Be careful, Wyatt!" Amalie shouted. "I can't watch," she turned around, covering her face.

"We've arrived!" Steve said merrily. "Just you wait until the storm clears," he said with a nod of personal approval.

The storm disappeared almost as quickly as it had come, leaving behind a bright blue afternoon. We warmed ourselves on the boat deck and watched more than one rainbow stretch over the island.

"It doesn't get better than this," Wyatt said.

"Hello?" I heard Amalie say. I looked over to see how she was faring.

She was talking on her phone. "I got an email and I need to dispute these charges." I wondered who she was talking to. She had gracefully transitioned from typing out farewell messages to investigating a utility bill.

When she hung up, I asked, "Were you talking to Comcast?"

"Yea, I opened my email and saw this charge that didn't make sense," she answered.

"Amalie. *You* are nuts," I said.

"I am?"

"You were literally praying for your life twenty minutes ago and now you are disputing a cable bill."

She laughed, and it was her turn to shrug, "Who's up for snorkeling?"

She was a totally different person from the shivering POW I sat next to an hour ago. Off we went into the sea for a swim. After paddling around and chasing fish, we climbed back onto the boat to dry off. The rainbows had grown bigger and brighter, taking over the whole sky as if to match the intensity of the storm that birthed them.

"Dolphins!" Someone shouted, jumping up and down. "Come over here. I see dolphins. Two of them."

We scurried over to the side of the boat to see for ourselves. Grey fins poked out of the water every few seconds. One, then two, then three, then five. A pod of dolphins swam right by the boat. Exactly what we wanted, on an island to ourselves. Just not the way we had expected it.

What I experienced as an exhilarating adventure had been a doomsday scenario for Amalie. *Why?* If our thoughts shape our reality, what thoughts had raced through Amalie's mind? I would never know, but it didn't matter. Something fundamental was wrapped inside the question, waiting for me to notice it.

Whatever Amalie's thoughts were, they caught her attention and shifted her into a place of fear and stress. It wasn't the situation itself that was stressful, but her experience of her thoughts *about* the situation. She had been caught in a horror movie she had unwittingly written, directed, and starred in. Only she had the power to write a new movie, which she did the moment she felt safe—the high-stakes drama between her and Comcast. I was living in my thoughts, too, only mine had written a script of a high seas adventure.

I'm sure the thought of being thrown overboard crossed my mind, but I didn't believe it would happen, or that if it did, I would be fine.

Steve said the storm wouldn't last long, the water was warm, and I was a strong swimmer. Any thought of danger that floated in had floated right back out. A thought can float in and float out again without disturbing us, or it can completely throw us off balance. It all depends on how much we *believe* the thought is true. Not only had Amalie experienced thoughts of her mortality, but she also had *believed* them. If Amalie hadn't believed she was in danger, she could have gotten up and danced with me or sat back and admired the storm. Amalie quickly shifted to *believing* she was safe once we docked the boat. This change instantly impacted her behavior: she went from cowering in her boyfriend's lap to disputing her cable bill.

I mentally tucked this realization away, saving it for a future moment when I might find myself plagued by fear. Fear has swallowed me whole, whether for just an instant right before stepping on stage to speak or stretching on endlessly as I listen to alarming news cycles that the world is unsafe. The next time I got swept up in fear, I hoped I might have the space to remember that I was simply mesmerized by a belief.

There is a difference between having a thought and believing in the thought. We've collapsed the whole process of consciousness by forgetting that thinking and believing are two separate mechanisms. We even substitute the word *believe* with the word *think* all the time. I know I do. I say things like, "I think we're out of milk," and "I think those tickets are too expensive," and "I think it's going to rain later." What I mean is that I *believe* we are out of milk. I thought about it, and because I believe it, I'm going to do something about it. I'll get in my car and go to the store, head to the milk aisle and pick out a white carton with a little cow picture on it. I'll probably pick up some eggs and yogurt while I'm there. We only believe *some* of our thousands of thoughts, and those are the ones we focus on; they become the guiding forces that create our lives.

With my legs hanging over the edge of the sun-drenched boat, I realized that I might have quit the law, but the law never quit me. I had my own laws—internal contracts I'd made with myself. Inside my mind lived a stack of agreements I had signed onto about what's true. It works like this. A thought comes in and instantaneously I decide if I believe in it. The process is lightning fast, and I don't even realize I do it most of the time. If I believe the thought is true, I sign the contract. I put my name right there on the dotted line, giving the thought power and adding it to the stack I live my life by.

Empty words are things we say that we don't believe. They are the agreements we don't sign, and they have no power. *We* don't give them any power. On the boat I didn't believe any thoughts about being in danger, so they had no power over me. I *believed* I was safe, so I had fun. Because Amalie believed that she was in danger, she experienced fear and stress. Neither perspective was right or wrong, but both had the power to create our experiences because we believed them.

The power of thoughts as a creative force truly lies in our willingness to put our *belief* in them, to sign on the dotted line. There are two excellent gems here. The first is that our thoughts are not inherently true. They are not true simply because they exist. They are not anything except a formless series of words inside our heads. It's this other process called belief that's the kicker. If, and only if, we freely give our belief to our thought, *then* it becomes true. (Subjectively.) And don't forget that it's always up to *us* to decide what we believe. Amalie could tell me all day long that we were in danger, but I wasn't about to budge, and vice versa.

The second gem is that, like a contract, we can always renegotiate what we believe. We can cross out our signature and refuse to live by its terms. What we believe is allowed to change. As Amalie showed me, we already do this. In the blink of an eye, she went from cowering in fear to snorkeling. The difference now was that I understood how this process worked, I could *choose* to renegotiate instead of waiting for life's circumstances to do it for me.

What we believe impacts everything about who we think we are, what we are capable of, and how we show up in the world in each and every moment. I toiled away at a law firm even though I was unhappy because I believed I was supposed to. I dieted and struggled and cried as I stepped on the scale because I believed I needed to lose ten pounds to be beautiful. I took the chair in the back of the room and kept quiet as a mouse because I didn't believe I had anything important to contribute. I had been fumbling in the dark, creating my life unconsciously. But now that I knew about the power of thought, the tables turned. I was aware of my creative power. This power is our birthright, our privilege, and our responsibility. No one can create your life for you.

You are now and forevermore a conscious creator of your universe. Some call this God. I call it empowerment, and an absolute delight.

MILESTONES

INNER GUIDANCE

- ⥃ Thoughts are neither innately true nor powerful.
- ⥃ Thoughts have power when we believe in them.
- ⥃ Only we have the privilege and responsibility of deciding what we believe.
- ⥃ We always have the power to change what we believe.
- ⥃ The thoughts we believe shape our lives.

DEEPER NAVIGATION

1. Over the next week, notice when you feel strong emotions, both positive and negative. What were you thinking at the time? Notice how much credibility you gave these thoughts.
2. Write down some of your internal agreements. To spark your brainstorming, ask what you believe is true in different categories, such as family, career, health, finance, spirituality, recreation, friendships, and community.
3. Do you notice any patterns in your internal agreements? Which agreements cause you to feel hope? Fear? Confidence? Frustration?
4. Notice how your internal agreements influence your behavior. As your awareness of your own internal agreements heightens, notice how everyone is acting based on their own internal agreements.

6

I AM CREATIVE

Danielle in Leros, Greece (2018)

The tiny Greek isle of Leros sits a few miles from the Turkish coast and boasts a population of 8,500. Tourism has barely touched its shores. It has no fancy bells and whistles to attract droves of summer sun-seekers. Our host's mother, Ama, picked us up at the island's school cafeteria-sized airport. Stepping off the plane, the air was thick with olive oil from the groves dotting the island.

"We go to food," Ama explained.

From my previous messages with our host, I knew she would take us to a grocery store to stock up on supplies before showing us our digs for the next two weeks. I nodded and smiled, and Ted echoed "Great!" as we piled into her beat-up Fiat Punto.

Once on the road, she made a fist with her right hand and twisted it up and down.

"Okay?" She asked. I looked at Ted, clueless this time. He gave her a thumbs-up and turned around in the front passenger's seat to tell me, "We're picking up a scooter to get around the island."

I raised my eyebrows and asked gently, "Did you get an international driver's license?" I was pretty sure I knew the answer.

Ted shrugged his shoulders and turned back around in his seat, implying that he hadn't but that he didn't think it would stop us from getting a scooter. That was still our dynamic, regardless of how much I shed my devotion to rules. I would have gotten the license, as it was one thing I could control to ensure things would work out. Ted hadn't even considered that they wouldn't work out. I suppose if I had really been concerned, I would have gotten the license myself. I straddled both worlds, somewhere between lining up my ducks in a row as best I could while surrendering to the belief that everything would work out.

The hillside apartment was perfect, no frills but great Wi-Fi and an unbeatable view of the sea. It had that quintessential European crumbling grandness to it. A linoleum floor opened up to a cracked stone patio with plastic folding chairs and a marble coffee table set into a wrought iron frame. I plopped down on a chair and tossed my airplane water bottle down on the marble tabletop. The crinkled plastic felt too cheap for such a grand platform, so I poured it into a ceramic mug from the kitchen. Sprawled out on my lawn chair, I took a note from the sea that effortlessly kept the boats in the harbor afloat and relaxed. Towards the horizon the island curved to the right, creating a little inlet with a hidden beach dotted with scrubby bushes and a few white houses that climbed the distant hill. Beyond the inlet and out further into the sea was a hazy brown mound that I thought must be another island, or perhaps even Turkey.

After digging through our bags to find our toothbrushes and fresh clothes, we drove down the road to grab some dinner at a little restaurant that overlooked the water. Our first meal was a feast of *souvlaki* (skewered meat and veggies), mussels, *labneh* (strained yogurt), eggplant, and cheese. The wind was light and warm. I was happy.

A few days later we visited Panetelli beach, a little pebbly inlet north of our house about two minutes by scooter. Never having ridden a scooter before, we had managed to rent one with about 50 ccs of power for ten euros a day. The guy who rented it to us kept a straight face the entire time, and only later did we discover it was not nearly powerful enough to carry two grown adults up any sort of incline. The engine groaned as the lizards passed us by. I'd get off and walk a couple of meters until the road was flat again and I could hop back on. I think it was the only type of scooter we could rent without that driver's license.

Panetelli beach was slightly touristy, meaning it had a hotel the size of a modest home and three cafes. My kind of touristy. A tourist boat, the Barbarossa, was scheduled to leave that afternoon for a sail around the aptly named White Rock Islands and snorkeling at Arki Island. With nothing better to do and nowhere else to be, we boarded the boat along with ten other travelers from all over the world.

At sea without a cell signal, Ted and I started chatting about human evolution. It started innocently enough. He was wearing his Garmin watch, which tracked his exercise, heart rate, sleep quality, and stress level. He had developed a keen interest in wearable technology that offered unparalleled access to personal health and wellness data. Not only into physical health, he also dove into all kinds of newly-fashionable wearable tech that offered insights into his mental and emotional states, monitored his nervous system, and provided exercises and practices to bring down his stress levels and create calm. Heralded as the future of evolution in human performance, leading-edge tech had become his passion. I suggested he might want to take it off and store it safely while on the boat.

I had never been quite as into data and metrics as Ted. Perhaps this is because I am internally motivated and don't like being pushed to exercise by an alert on my wrist, or because I am totally fine with a gut check to test how well I sleep or if I'm stressed. Squeezing all the data from our bodies into one metric seemed more limiting than if I simply tuned into myself. Plus, my burgeoning understanding of thoughts as the creative source of life amplified my internal approach, although I loved witnessing Ted's passion and seeing human potential through his eyes.

"What will tech like this enable humans to do in the future? What limits will it stretch?" I asked.

Squinting into the sun, Ted answered, "Anything. We will be able to dial in and accomplish things better, faster, and longer than ever before."

I leaned into the ocean spray to cool off from the summer heat. "You mean like running faster marathons?"

"Sure, definitely. Also healing ourselves from injury faster and easier. Preventing illness altogether."

I nodded along. I was certainly a fan of a more empowered, personalized approach to our wellness, and this tech offered us a way to give ourselves back some of the power we had unwittingly given away to our health care system.

"Do you think we need all this tech to evolve this way?" I wondered out loud. As much as I loved the tech, it wasn't essential for me.

"It's pushing the direction of our wellness progress," he answered. "I'm not sure we'd grow this way without it."

The wood bench of the boat was starting to chafe my thighs and I rummaged through my bag for a towel to put under my legs. It gave me a moment to gather my thoughts. "I think of tech as a bridge, allowing us to reach beyond what we believe is possible. Once we cross the bridge, our beliefs about what is possible will have stretched. But it's not the tech that stretches us. The tech seems to give us permission to stretch."

We had moved into familiar territory: Ted focused externally while I focused internally. Whereas he looked outwards and saw the world being created, I looked inward. I suppose that's why he dove headfirst into all this tech while I thought of it as a companion to the evolution of human cosmology. Chuckling, Ted flipped his sunglasses off his forehead and wiped the beads of sweat that formed where the glasses nuzzled his skin. But I wasn't done yet.

"Do you think humans can regrow limbs? Can we live forever?" I asked as I stared off into the horizon, a little intimidated to meet Ted's gaze with these seemingly far-fetched questions.

Quite easily he answered, "No. It's not in our DNA."

Is that true? I wondered. I knew little about human DNA and Ted had been pre-med in college, so I tended to defer to his competency in such matters. It seemed true. If our DNA did present such possibilities, it would be flashing all over the news ticker. "Starfish can regrow limbs and they don't have nearly as complex DNA as humans, so maybe it's something our biology can evolve to do," I mused.

"That's exactly why they can regrow limbs. Their genetics aren't as complex as ours. There aren't as many things that can go wrong, or as many things that need to go exactly right."

I pushed, "What about our stem cells? Can't they be used to create any part of the body?"

"Yes," he replied. "But we don't have any of those when we are adults. They are all spoken for, assigned to some function by the time we are born."

"That makes sense," I sighed. Ted and his silver tongue were quite convincing. After all, he knew what a compelling argument looked like. If I were basing my foundation for this conversation on what I knew about biology, which is very little, that would have been the end of the conversation.

"At least let's agree that there is a way for living organisms to regrow their limbs. It's not unheard of."

"Sure," Ted agreed. He wasn't as rigid in his position as I sometimes liked to paint him. "And there are jellyfish that are immortal if we are talking about dying. And tardigrades can technically live forever."

"What's a tardigrade?" I was constantly fascinated by how much my husband knew about the world. His ability to consume and remember information far outpaced my own.

"Those cute space bears," Ted reminded me, as he made a small growling noise for the bear-like microscopic creatures. Not long ago he had shown me an article about tardigrades that had the capacity within their one millimeter-sized bodies to suspend animation and even survive in space.

"Oh, yes!" I rocked back on my seat with delight. "So, intelligence already knows how to extend life seemingly forever, and to regrow pieces of the body."

Our boat sailed closer to the White Rocks Island, a small oasis in the crystal blue sea with a beach made of small slick white stones, worn by the water and perfect for skipping.

"So why not humans?" I asked again.

43

Scratching at the prickles of wood fraying on the beam of this old boat, Ted offered me his science-based reasons as to why not humans. "Based on what we've seen, based on what we've tested, based on what we know to be true regarding human genetics, it's just not possible."

"Is it fair to say that *you* don't believe it's possible, but it may be possible?" I tried again. I was like the judge, striking with questions from every angle to test his argument.

"I don't think so. Science would have to jump to some implausible conclusions and it's nowhere near indicating that it will. The world is quite organized, and it would be a strange bending of what we know to be true to get to a place where humans live forever or start regrowing arms and legs."

"Yeah, I see what you mean." I thought I did anyway. I tried to put his words in my perspective, "When you look at our *physicality*, it's not in the cards."

"Right. Technology can't evolve us past our physical limitations. There is a limit to what we can do."

"Can we live to 150?" I pressed with a different tactic.

"Yes, that is likely."

Okay, he bit. Curious how far I could stretch this, I asked if we could live to 200. Yes. 250? Yes, likely so. 300?

"If the other things on the planet don't go sideways, like global warming, and our tech supports us living quality lives, then yes. It's a slow-down of senescence, the process where our cells stop functioning, so any tech that slows or reverses this process can extend our lifespan," he answered.

I continued delicately, "What about 500?"

"Yes, humans can evolve to live a much longer life span, but not forever."

"I see." But I didn't see. Where would he draw the line? I wasn't sure, but what I did understand was that he *believed* we could not completely evolve past senescence.

"What do you think?" he asked. Eyeing the island that was fully in view, Ted's quick calculus indicated we had about five minutes before it was time to snorkel; he was eager to hear how my wheels were spinning.

I took a deep breath. I was a little scared to say this out loud, as I had never expressed my thoughts on this before. I had only come around to this belief myself and giving it voice made me feel vulnerable. (I was still practicing unwinding that understanding my perspective didn't require agreeing with it.)

"Humans can definitely live forever," I said. "We can definitely regrow our limbs the same as we can heal a wound." As the words came out of my mouth, I heard how crazy I sounded. I imagined everyone at my law firm raising their eyebrows and whispering to each other that I had fallen off the deep end. Maybe I should throw myself overboard now.

Ted didn't blink.

"I don't think it has much to do with our physicality or our DNA. It's all mutable. I don't think anyone could have guessed that single-celled creatures would become dinosaurs or wombats or humans. Part of biology is evolution—meaning our DNA *can* change. In fact, change is written into our DNA. Nothing in our biology makes me believe that it's not possible. Evolution always seems to come down to how an organism can thrive more effectively. All this incredible tech is a hook that pulls and stretches what we believe we are capable of, expanding our capacity to thrive. The tech is certainly an accelerant, inviting more and more people to expand what they believe is possible for the human species, but for me it looks like the source of our evolution is our beliefs, and there's no limit to what we can believe. The most important tech we can focus on is our human operating system."

I was on a roll. Although Ted mostly disagreed with me, he listened. And he found things he could nod along with. "You're talking about the hundredth monkey phenomenon," he offered.

The hundredth monkey effect came out of a 1980s study of monkeys that lived on an island off the coast of Japan. They had learned to wash their food to clean it of unwanted sand and dirt. The monkeys watched and imitated each other so the novel idea started to spread across the island. Once a hundred monkeys knew the practice, it tipped the field of awareness and suddenly all the monkeys had this incredible knowledge. It's the same thing as when you have a bright idea and suddenly so does your friend or colleague, seemingly independent of each other.

"Exactly," I agreed. "We don't know where the tipping point is for human consciousness, whether it's a million people or a billion people. But we do see that more and more people are extending what they believe is physically and biologically possible. There are documentaries about people who refused to believe their limitations. When doctors told them they'd be paralyzed for the rest of their lives, they taught themselves to walk, or healed themselves from cancer when Western medicine failed them. The belief that humans are capable of more than we currently understand is already out there and momentum is picking up. Living forever and regrowing limbs may seem too far afield now, but not too long ago so did using meditation and visualization to heal a broken back. For me, our evolution all starts with what we believe."

It was simple for me: thoughts are creative forces. What we believe becomes the framework for our reality, and we can create whatever we believe we can create. And we can *only* create what we believe. Like gravity, this rule has no exceptions. Unlike man-made rules that include carve-outs, there are none for the fundamental laws of the universe that I had come to know.

This was a principle that so many people already knew, although perhaps in a much more intimate context. If I had a nickel for every time I heard the phrase "self-limiting belief," I could afford a front row seat on Elon Musk's rocket to Mars. What is a self-limiting belief other than something we *believe* that is getting in the way of our experience of what is beyond that belief? To live more of what we know is possible, we must be willing to revoke our consent to beliefs that hold us back. This process of expanding our belief system is universal, applicable even in the most far-out situations. We create what we believe we can create, whether that's the love of a supportive family, financial stability, or living forever.

After leaving a constricting career, I wanted to create a life in which I felt the spaciousness of possibility. I craved to understand that anything was possible. Learning that my limiting beliefs were not necessarily true was cause for celebration and I danced with joy for a long time. I stretched my beliefs as far as I could imagine, like living forever.

For some time, getting acquainted with limitless possibility was more than enough, but eventually the question changed. I transitioned from wondering what is possible, to asking *if anything is possible, what do I want to do?* How do I want to *use* my creative power? This was quite a daunting question, but what I had learned was that there was no rush to find the answer, and that the answer was waiting within me.

MILESTONES

INNER GUIDANCE

- Our beliefs create the universe of what is possible.
- We create what we believe we can create.
- A self-limiting belief is something we think is true that forms a boundary for what we experience.
- We usually talk about self-limiting beliefs in the context of our personal lives, yet it is universally applicable. The context and content of our beliefs are irrelevant to the mechanisms of how we create our reality.

DEEPER NAVIGATION

1. Refer back to the internal agreements you brainstormed in Chapter 5. Which ones feel true? Which ones do not feel true anymore? Cross out the agreements are not true anymore.
2. Reflect on the boundaries created by your internal agreements. How do they expand what's possible? How do they create limitations?
3. If you could wave a magic wand and stretch a belief beyond its current boundary, what would it be? Do this for every internal agreement that feels limiting. Cross out your old internal agreements.
4. Look at your new list of internal agreements. This list consists of beliefs that feel true and feel more expansive than ever before! Keep this list handy and come back to it regularly to review these questions again and again. Your list is dynamic, alive, and ever changing.

~ PART II ~

ENERGY

Someday, after mastering the winds, the waves, the tides and gravity, we shall harness for God the energies of love, and then, for a second time in the history of the world, man will have discovered fire.

—PIERRE TEILHARD DE CHARDIN

7

I AM DESIRE

Uluru, Australia (2018)

I sat on a red mountain in a sea of dust. As the early morning sun rose, the mountain changed hues from tea rose to crimson, terra cotta, and vermilion. Uluru, the sandstone behemoth in the Australian outback, beckoned me. Ted had flown to Switzerland to help run the first ever crypto event in Davos during the World Economic Forum, while I joined up with a friend and hopped over to the land down under. We arrived in Sydney and drove the Gold Coast, stopping at all the glistening beaches and taking photos of every kangaroo that dotted the landscape like deer. But Uluru called us to dive deeper into the country's earthy energy.

Uluru is sacred to the Anangu, Australia's Aboriginal people. For the Anangu, and many others, Uluru is considered the heart of Australia and the spiritual center of the world, known for opening visitors' hearts. According to Anangu legend, Uluru was created at the beginning of time by ancestral beings who formed the otherwise featureless world and who created all living things. Australian settlers later took Uluru for their own, only recently giving the land back to the Anangu. The Anangu initially refused to lay claim to the land, as they believed the sacred site could not be owned by anyone.

In the middle of Australia's summer, we drove the long stretch of hazy desert road to Uluru. With reports of the extreme heat melting the asphalt, we armed ourselves with extra jugs of water and gas, just in case. Ted made me swear I'd be cautious not to wind up as dingo bait.

We arrived at a popular hostel for tourists with about a dozen small brown structures each packed with bunk beds formed in a hodge-podge pattern around a central bathroom. Guests pass down tips to the newcomers, and after hearing a high-pitched yelp across the patchy grass, we were informed to always look inside our hiking boots before putting them on our feet. You never knew what creature might take refuge in the shade of a boot toe. Weren't Australian bugs the largest and scariest? My stomach curled at the thought of losing a pinky to a gigantic Australian scorpion and I made my friend promise he'd accompany me at night if I needed to walk to the bathroom.

That evening we toured the edges of Uluru to see Field of Light, an art installation by Bruce Munro, who had been inspired by the rock. As the sun set, Uluru faded into silhouette and the ground beneath the rock came alive. Over 50,000 spindles of light woke up like luminous flowers that bloom in secret for the moon. Shades of purple, blue, white, and orange erupted from the desert floor. With the sun dipping behind us, the installation of light flowers illuminated the hallowed ground at the foot of Uluru, and I lost myself in its mystery as I meandered through the field of color.

By seven the next morning it was already nearing 40 degrees Celsius (104°F) as we drove to see Uluru burst into its own colorful splendor with the sunrise. I climbed up a few feet of the rock and sat in its shadow, seeking protection from the sun. I readied myself for what I hoped would be a transformative meditation. After all, I was smack in the middle of all this mystical energy. I pulled my hood up over my head and covered my ears with my hands to block the mosquitos from buzzing their way inside. Not an ideal meditation posture, but preferable to tiny wings fluttering inside my ear canals. Breathe in, settle down, and take off . . .

What's that noise? Gravel crunching. I opened my eyes and saw a few tourists walking the path nearby. *No problem*, I thought. *I can wait for them to leave. Okay, breathe in, settle down . . .*

A couple of women sat under a treasured spot of shade a few feet away and started chatting in Japanese. No problem. I'd wait for them to move on. More footsteps, more crunching, more talking, more buzzing. Now I was frustrated. Here I was trying to meditate and all these people were getting in my way! I couldn't even remember my mantra. I took a deep breath to move my frustration out and the Voice popped into my head.

"Danielle," it greeted me sternly.

"Now what? I am trying to make the distractions disappear, not hear more of them."

"I know, but hear me out," the Voice said. "Stop getting frustrated by the people."

Telling someone to stop how they are feeling is famous for creating the opposite effect. But this was my Voice talking to me. I trusted it. I mentally rolled my eyes and said, "Okay, but easier said than done."

"Not really," my Voice continued. "Just stop. This is not your private rock. Uluru doesn't belong to you. Isn't that what you learned about its history? Celebrate whatever inspired people to come here today. Trust that they are here to get as much from their experience as you are, whether they are meditating or chatting or picking their noses. Stop feeling frustrated, stop seeing the other people as impediments. Embrace them as part of this experience and get on with your meditation."

"Oh, I see." And I did. My Voice had a way of speaking to me that was direct and compassionate and a little sassy. All my distracting thoughts about the mosquitos and the tourists had caught my attention like waves crashing on the shore. I thought the goal of my meditation was to stop the waves, stop thinking, and enter that blissful, clear mind that everyone raves about. But thoughts kept coming, flowing in and flowing out. Thoughts about how loud gravel is, thoughts about how hard it is to hear my thoughts. My Voice told me to let them float on by and relax into the space underneath, where the water is deep and calm.

I exhaled out my frustration and the noises faded as if I were sinking beneath the surface of the water. My meditation was fine, but I don't remember it to be particularly powerful. The experience wasn't about meditation anymore. It wasn't about clearing the mind and waiting patiently in silence for wisdom. I expected my Voice would offer me "aha" moments once I made space for them, but it pointed me towards something else entirely—the space itself. It offered no revelatory ideas or insights, but something much more intimate and more valuable than anything else in the entire world.

In knowing this space, I would know myself.

What is this space underneath our thoughts? What lives in the cosmic tango between mind and matter? Our inner spark of sentience. Our *us-ness*. It's been called many names: intuition, inner wisdom, soul, spirit, instinct, innate intelligence, God, inner voice, loving awareness, inner being, *chi*, energy, *prana*, life force, and the list goes on. While these labels all have slightly different connotations, they all point to the same place— the non-physical force and dominant energy of who we are.

I picture this space like a love letter. To travel across the world to its recipient, it needs to be placed inside an envelope. Tucked inside, the content of the letter is safe. As the letter is handled by the post office, knocked about in bins, and shipped across the planet, the envelope endures some wear. Its corners might soften and the address might smudge. It could arrive a bit dingy, stained, and spotted. Every so often along the trip we wipe away the smudges, peel off worn out stickers, and brush off the crumbs left by whoever was eating a croissant while handling the post.

The envelope might arrive looking quite used. Like the envelope, our interactions with the world leave an imprint on us, and they wind up traveling with us throughout our lives. Our experiences leave their marks—the dents and scars and frayed edges. But our experiences only impact the envelope, while inside is the most exquisite love letter. The wear of travel hasn't damaged the letter, and it can't change what the letter says. Its whispers of desire can't be erased, warped, or worn out. The words remain the same as the day the letter was lovingly placed inside the envelope. And the envelope is grateful, as the letter gifted it purpose.

This love letter is who we are underneath it all. It is our *desire* to experience life—*our* life. This desire is our birthright. This is not desire

54

sourced from our ego that echoes the wants of our psychological structures and social roles. This desire is not at all concerned with your weight or how many zeros are in your bank account. This desire is a *force*, a never-ending and never-yielding thrumming inside our chests. It's the fire that burns within us, an eternal flame fueled by the sunrise. This force is a key, a map, and a prophecy. It is a well of wisdom available to guide us through each moment of our lives, the highs and the lows, the molehills and the mountains.

Sitting quietly on that hot rock, desire swelled in my chest. Once I unhooked my attention from all my thoughts, whatever they were, I felt desire. Desire to experience the experience. Or as Ram Dass would put it, to *be here now*.

We may get distracted by our efforts to clean our envelope of stuck gum and tattered corners, but the letter remains inside, intact, ready and waiting for us to read it. The power of connecting to our inner love letter is that it offers us the most potent, efficient, and dynamic GPS for life. It knows who we were before the outside world told us who to be. Before we agreed to play by its rules. Because the outside world can't warp our desire, it stays true to us. Our love letters offer us the singular, extraordinary wisdom of who we really are.

There is a love letter tucked inside each of us, and it will never offer false guidance. Our inner wisdom is incorruptible, unflappable, and unyielding. Neither body nor mind can interfere with it. It cannot be knocked off course. It will never advise us to play small or wait it out. It will never deny us our truth, and it will always navigate us towards this truth. This space is where we should go when we feel confused, frustrated, lost, and disconnected. This is the place that connects us to our calm, our clarity, our confidence to move through the world. This is the place we access when we put down our water bottles and let the clear water rise above the sandy thoughts.

It is up to us to trust this force. In each moment, our Voice is nudging us in the direction of satisfaction and fulfillment. It may be a sweet and simple whisper to enjoy a cup of coffee in the sunshine. It may not make sense in the moment, and it may pull us in a direction that we can't explain to our friends and family. They may ask *why*, and you can only answer *because I desire it.* Let that be enough. Let that be more than enough. And remember that all we can really understand is one step at a time. Anything more than that is an illusion, a trick of our minds that seek the comfort of a completely laid out plan. When we connect to the wisdom of our desire, we access the most efficient guidance system there is to create the life we yearn for, one step at a time.

This letter was where I was truly traveling—both in meditation and in life. All the amazing "aha" moments of insight I had received while sitting in reflection were the pillars for *something*, and the something was *how* to open the envelope and read my letter. Once I read it, I understood. Everything I do comes from desire. Desire never stops. It never ceases to live inside the beat of my heart. It's my muse, my teacher, and my pilot.

MILESTONES

INNER GUIDANCE

- ⮞ Underneath our thoughts is the most dominant aspect of who we are: a force of desire.
- ⮞ We are all gifted the desire to live our life. There's no right or wrong way to do this. Period.
- ⮞ In this space underneath our minds lives who we truly are, unchanged by the outside world.
- ⮞ This is our inner wisdom, and it offers us an alternative source to seek answers.
- ⮞ Our inner wisdom is incorruptible, unflappable, and unyielding. Neither body nor mind can interfere with it. It cannot be knocked off course.
- ⮞ Consequently, our inner wisdom is our most efficient and effective guidance system. It will always offer us the next step forward to navigate our lives.
- ⮞ Our inner wisdom is always calling to us; it is up to us to listen.

DEEPER NAVIGATION

1. What does it mean to you to feel fully connected to yourself? When did you last feel this way? Notice the circumstances that allow you to feel connected—the who, what, when, where, why, and how. Look for any patterns that offer insight into your connection to your inner wisdom.

2. Notice when you feel pulled away from self-connection. What happened? A thought floats in, grabs your attention, and takes you with it. Try to observe when this happens and notice the process. Practice witnessing the thought float by without being pulled away from your self-connection.

8

I AM YOU

Danielle and Ted in Singapore (2017)

"Where are you from?" is the most common question we ask each other upon introduction, and it was starting to drive me nuts. I was asked that question everywhere we went, and I'd answer, "the U.S." with a tone of apology. Apology for its shortcomings, apology for my privilege. The question always took me out of the moment. I could be laughing with a new friend over a bowl of noodles and then, bam! I'm no longer across the table from you; I'm across the world. I'm no longer me; I'm the representation of all the baggage that comes with my answer. Then I'd struggle to right the ship and guide us back to *the moment*. To be here, now, together. My heartache over this simple question inspired me to take a deeper look at my answer. While it was true, it somehow felt wrong.

We arrived at the uniquely clean carnival called Singapore—a sanitary bonanza of tastes, colors, smells, soaring heights, and tucked away bridges behind groves of glowing forests. Everything was user-friendly and it was easy to get around. There were plenty of skyscrapers, but it wasn't claustrophobic in the way that New York City tightens my chest. The buildings in Singapore are glass with multi-story topiaries and gardens jutting out from all angles and heights. The meticulously planned architecture integrated organic life into the swooping curves of the buildings and skywalks that connect them. Everyone moved in the harmony designed by the landscape.

Just as dazzling were the hawker centers with their endless rows of food stalls that punched the air with scents of Little India, Chinatown, and Middle Eastern delights. The food reflected the people that breathed life into this country—Indian, Malay, Chinese, Arab, Buddhist, Christian, Muslim, Hindu—all living, working, and breaking naan together. One afternoon, Ted and I took a stroll down Arab Street where we ate mouth-watering *murtabak*, a pan-fried flat bread folded over and stuffed with chicken. Licking our fingers, we continued our walk and explored the patchwork of storefronts and medley of cultures that careened into each other—a burger restaurant run by black Indian Australians; a Swedish restaurant called Fike with the tagline "Halal - authentically Swedish"; and an Italian gelato spot with Turkish coffee next door to a Persian rug store with a Chinese clerk. Each place was born from its own ethnic roots, and all soared with Singaporean wings.

How did all these people answer where they were from?

Ted always included in his answer that he is Canadian. (He is.) Ted is from a Jewish immigrant family and has always felt like an outsider. We were traveling during the Trump presidency and Ted would say he didn't identify with what America stood for, not wanting to be mistaken for someone who supported Trump's policies. This desire to unhitch himself from American politics was especially true when we traveled to places whose democratically elected leaders had been "substituted" with puppets of the American agenda.

I understood his desire. Many of us have an issue with the increasing polarization of the American populace around social matters, enough to make us wince at answering "I'm from the United States" without offering a qualifier. I also feel like an "other" in an America painted with a brush dipped in light beer, Monday-night football, and super-sized ignorance. On one hand, I feel rejected by America for my otherness and, on the other, I am relieved to escape being "American" for all its shortcomings.

I was raised on the idea that America stands for freedom. It's part of my DNA. If you ask a hundred Americans what it means to be an "American," you'll get a hundred different answers. That's what the U.S. is about—the freedom to answer in any way you want, to be whoever you want, to value whatever you want. America is a collection of different ideas—a story about freedom as well as revolution, slavery, isolationism, hope, colonialism, greed, deceit, power, truth, collaboration, invention, education, ignorance, love, fear, genocide, exploration, liberation, and family.

The collection of ideas that make up America is not set in stone. America is ever-changing, evolving with each generation. The young know they have the power to effect change. This is the hope and joy that the young gift their homeland, which sadly is often waved off as naiveté. Each person carries America forward in their story, transforming it, chronicling what it means to be part of an American community, part of the American culture. Each adds their own perspective, memories, relationships, love, laughter, triumphs, and pain. The way each of us chooses to move through the world changes the collective consciousness of our homeland, one person at a time, one generation at a time. I am unbelievably proud to contribute to America's evolution. By adding my story about what it means to be American, I breathe light into dark places.

Yet, as I traveled the globe, it still didn't feel completely right to say, "I'm from America." I was perfectly satisfied to have been born there, to have grown up there, to have been educated there, and to eventually raise a family there. In college I double majored in politics and American studies. What was my hesitation in identifying as American?

I didn't want to be responsible for carrying historical shame and broken hope into my story, but that's not where my nagging feeling of discomfort came from. I knew that no matter how much I may not have wanted to identify with America, there was no use denying it. The cognitive dissonance rattling around in my body was assuaged by a simple reminder that being American was still only a label, a construct of the mind. I may have wanted it to be the most beautiful, loving label in my power, but it was still an identifier that separated me from others.

Our collective American consciousness is only one piece of the whole of humanity. We are all human. We all experience love and fear, pain and triumph. And yet we find ourselves categorizing and labeling, boxing and sorting. We have disengaged from connecting with each other because we are sure that we are different, and differences tend to invoke fear, to shut borders, to close the heart.

Fear and hate are mind-made.

This is the teaching of the great spiritual and religious masters: love thy neighbor as thyself; do unto others as you would have them do unto you. What I've come to understand is that the less that I define myself, the more available I am to everyone else. The less that I live in a box of labels, the more everyone else becomes available to me. Our ability to connect deeply with another has nothing to do with our minds. We've all seen moments of this universal, transcendental connection—a young black man cutting the lawn for a disabled white senior citizen; a child in a refugee camp with his arm outstretched, offering a bottle of water to a soldier standing guard; a group of strangers working together on a beach to rescue a stranded whale. We let go of our nationality, race, gender—all the labels that separate us—and find our humanity, the place where one soul touches another. Being labeled as "American" is irrelevant to the soul.

I simultaneously feel proud to be from America and reject it as an answer to where I'm from. It's true, but incomplete. It's correct on one level, but not the level that I live on. The next time I'm asked where I am from, I'll place my hand over my heart and say, "I'm from here. From the heartland."

And so are you.

MILESTONES

INNER GUIDANCE

- ↭ The labels that we use to define and describe ourselves are stories—constructs that live in the mind. They do not apply to the deeper part of who we are.
- ↭ If we peel away our labels and constructs, we also peel away the illusion of our differences. What we find underneath is the love letter that lives in everyone.
- ↭ The energy of desire lives in each of us. When we focus on this level, we invite connection, compassion, and love.

DEEPER NAVIGATION

1. People typically relate to each other by comparing our envelopes, or labels. For example, balding men may notice Bob's full head of hair and think of him as "Bob with the good hair," and tall men may notice how short he is and think of him as "short Bob," and single women may notice his wedding ring and think of him as "married Bob." Notice that how you choose to identify yourself influences how you relate to others.

2. As you observe more of your own identity constructs, your awareness of others' constructs will heighten. Notice how other people relate to the world through their own identities. Notice when you share the same construct as someone else, and how that influences your relationship. For example, perhaps two bald men both bond over harbored jealousy towards Bob because they both perceive him as "Bob with the good hair."

3. Trying to relate to someone whose constructs are vastly different may be difficult and stressful. Practice sinking beneath the constructs to see their love letters instead. What becomes available here?

9

I AM UNIVERSAL

Cloud Castle in Santa Elena, Colombia (2018)

The early morning fog slowly curled up the side of the mountain as it rose with the sun, coming in through the open windows of my house like exploring fingers. Every afternoon arrived with the promise of a thunderstorm. After I'd close my laptop and disconnect the Wi-Fi to prevent it from shorting out, all that was left to do was listen to the raindrops dancing on the roof and birds rustling the leaves on the trees, watch butterflies flutter away to dryer branches and lizards scramble under brush.

At 9,000 feet, I was living in the sky. Our house was called the Cloud Castle, built in the local ranchero style at the top of the mountain overlooking the city of Medellin in the Aburrá Valley of Colombia. It boasted a simple brick exterior, interior stained-glass windows and doors, and a wood fireplace that sat in the middle of the living room. Suspended over the mountainside was the second level, an entirely glass-walled room filled with yoga mats and meditation cushions that offered an uninterrupted view over the mountain. At night Ted would wrap me in his arms as we lay on a thick cushion, gazing at the twinkling stars that dotted the ink black sky, a mirror reflecting the dazzling valley of city lights.

There were two lampposts along the path from the Cloud Castle to the Gingerbread House, the other house on the property. Succulents filled the lampposts, reminding me to allow the natural world to illuminate my way. I found myself constantly gravitating towards the enormous garden filled with veggies, herbs, beans, and a native tobacco plant. I'd sit at the picnic table near rows of cabbage and listen to crickets or watch a neighborhood kitten shyly pad around a favorite tree. My neighbor, a few hundred yards away, often listened to a Colombian radio station while he worked outside. The sound poured over, like someone shook a soda can full of Spanish soap operas and folk music and popped the top, spraying salsa, declarations of love, and fast-talking commercials for the best avocados in all directions.

Ted and I had been craving a month of solitude and a chance to connect with nature. Since leaving Washington D.C., my relationship with noise had changed. I needed more quiet. When I first moved to Dupont Circle, the everyday noises included ambulance sirens, the thump of the bass from the bar across the street, early morning beeps of garbage trucks, shouts from outside the front stoop, neighbors slamming doors shut, and on and on. The sounds of city life were magical. Oh, how I wanted to be in the middle of all the action! Hearing the noises of my Dupont Circle community confirmed my existence because I was *there* to hear it. Of course, the opposite was also true—and this was the most comforting part—the neighbors, bar-goers, and passersby could hear *my* noises. I contributed to the soundtrack of other people's lives. I needed to be part of the cacophony of the living.

My relationship to noise changed for two reasons. The whistle of the wind in the trees, the conversation of the birds, and the low rumble of thunder clouds eliminated the need to be heard. There was no one else to hear me. Physically removing myself from the cityscape showed me how refreshing the sounds of nature could be. I didn't need anything from them. More importantly was that by this point, I had peeled off enough layers of insecurity, and the need for external validation of Who I Am was softer. I no longer felt the compulsion to contribute to anyone else's soundtrack. I wanted to bask in the solitude of being with myself, listening to the sound of my Voice. The quiet that used to feel empty now felt full. Here in Santa Elena, I invited it to silently hold my hand.

After a long, cramped flight complete with delays, layovers, and stolen naps on metal airport benches, we drove up a winding mountain road to our house, tired and bedraggled. The moon hung in the trees and rain had started to fall. We dragged our wet bags inside and turned on the lights to survey our new home. It was called a castle, but it was rustic at best. I shivered in the cold as I looked around the open kitchen and living room. There was no HVAC system, no central air, no heat, no fans, no buttons to push or switches to flip. Cold, tired, and wet, Ted found a pile of pine and eucalyptus logs underneath the overhang of the house. Mostly dry, he carried them inside to the fireplace and got reacquainted with his boyhood fire-starting skills.

Meanwhile, my stomach rumbled and I scoped out the kitchen. I saw no conveniences. No microwave, no dishwasher, not even an oven. Certainly no air-fryer or Vitamix, waffle maker, or Keurig for a pick-me-up brew. In the corner a thirty-year-old fridge and an ice box stood next to a four-burner electric stove, a few wooden spatulas, some pots and pans, and luckily an electric kettle. If I didn't feel like using the stove to cook, there was no Uber Eats to deliver a hot meal while I flopped on the couch and watched Netflix. I wondered if I would make it a month here. I wanted quiet, but I also wanted comfort. I wasn't trying to prove I could make it in the wilderness.

In my cold, damp exhaustion, I fought back tears. I had made the wrong decision to come here. I wanted sushi and a hot shower. With no choice to scroll our phones for food delivery, we cooked our first meal of meat and rice on the stove, cleared the cobwebs from our bedroom and snuggled under the covers. Our cold toes rubbed against each other, hoping for a sunny, warm tomorrow.

It is amazing how fast we can acclimate. A few weeks later, I woke up in the middle of the night to pee. Sitting on the toilet, I blinked my blurry eyes open and saw a very large spider dangling not two feet away from my face. It had descended its silky rope and was engaged mid-battle with a big black scorpion. Coolly, I wished the spider luck as I flushed the toilet and padded back to the bedroom. The spider seemed a more accommodating roommate than the scorpion.

The chatter of birds woke me in the morning—an invitation to take a stroll outside and explore the property that I had rushed by in the cold darkness of the first evening. Every morning I was greeted by new life. In the tropical climate, it is always growing season and life cycles blend together. In a single breath, flowers bloomed and wilted; tree branches withered while others stretched into the sun. The circle of life happened all at once. I walked through the foliage, touching the petals and weaving into nature in any way I could. I wanted to connect.

"Before we came here," I said to Ted, "nature was picturesque, seen through a window or in a painting." Ted nodded while fanning the fire, his favorite new activity. "It was all about the view, you know? I wanted to enjoy a cup of coffee while soaking up the view of a mountain, a river, a forest, a nice backyard."

"Totally!" He agreed, although not sure where I was headed, his own focus turned toward the flame he was barely keeping alive in the damp wood. We really needed to keep a larger log pile inside the house since we knew it rained every afternoon.

"I still appreciate a good view, don't get me wrong," I continued. "But the view is separate and apart from us. We are here," I pointed down at my cozy-socked feet on the hardwood floor, "and the view is there," I concluded, pointing outside.

"Like these logs." Ted fanned the flame. "I created this fire with wood and air. It's simple, but deceptively so."

I nodded vigorously, hoping he'd explain himself without my prodding.

"I feel connected to the forest this way. I'm using the trees that are right here," he broke from fanning for a second to swivel towards the window where the pine and eucalyptus trees swayed in the breeze. "They are giving their energy to this fire, to create warmth for our comfort. And I am conducting the alchemy. It's so different from pushing a button for a gas fireplace and having the fire pop right on. You don't have to acknowledge the connection between you and your environment."

"Exactly!" I jumped off the kitchen stool. I had been drinking *agua panela*, a Colombian tea made with raw sugar naturally fortified with minerals, making the tea a somewhat healthy sweet treat. I headed back outside after kissing Ted on the forehead and on the hand that held the feather he used to fan the fire.

The feather had been on top of the fireplace when we arrived, signaling itself as the appropriate tool to use. Our host had connected us to our neighbors, folks who became fast friends and shepherded us through the customs of the rural community. One day they saw Ted waving the feather madly at the fire, pumping his arm up and down and creating more smoke than flame. Graciously, they showed us how a gentle flick of the wrist created wind with the natural motion of a bird in flight. Tuning into the elegant solutions of the natural world was exactly why we were in Santa Elena, and this new understanding of how to fan a fire with a feather was a gift of gold.

I sat at the wooden picnic table to gaze at all the life that sprang forth each day. Warm morning light filtered through the trees and cast a golden glow on the life that stretched out before me. Beyond the garden, the forest grew wild. Flowers bloomed everywhere—on bushes, poking straight up from the ground on thick individual stalks, and on the leaves of trees that painted the ground with pink and purple petals when it rained. The plants sent shoots of vibrant green leaves towards the sun. Flower buds blossomed in sweet exhale as the bees received their offerings.

A deeper appreciation of nature had stirred within me during an unscheduled stop in Hawaii on our way to Colombia. As East Coasters, Ted and I were used to folks going to Florida or Jamaica or Cancun for their tropical vacations. Hawaii seemed like the West Coast version, and we had no expectations beyond enjoying a new beach landscape. What we did have were dirt cheap tickets to an ocean-front villa on Maui.

Danielle at the black lava rocks in Maui (2018)

It turns out that Hawaii is not Florida, Mexico, or the Caribbean islands. Maui is an especially young island, formed a million years ago by the eruptions of the volcano Haleakalā. This soaring titan peeks into the stratosphere, inspiring the grandeur that architects strive for when they design towering cathedrals. It declares: God is here. The surrounding areas are dense with tropical forests and cascading waterfalls that seem to live in their own timeline. Bends in the quaint two-lane road revealed the sea lapping onto the shores of red, white, and black beaches. Wild waves crashed on massive, black, craggy lava rocks. Palm trees swayed in the ocean breeze and colorful birds cracked fruit in their beaks. There was magic in the atmosphere of a place left alone.

Minimally touched by man and technology, this tropical land overflows with primordial intelligence. Every leaf, insect, and grain of sand vibrates with the essence of life. Hawaii is not trying to be a tropical paradise to ease the souls of pale, stressed-out workaholics. It's not striving to keep its status as a top beach destination. Every rock, blade of grass, and drop of water vibrates with Mother Earth. She calls to us.

We were born from our Mother, and she draws us to her because she hosts our natural energy. The Earth is the womb of our species. She birthed us into being. She nourished us into thriving. She supported our exploration. She gave us food and warmth and guidance to evolve over millennia into the civilization we are today. We've unbound ourselves from our Mother by inventing tools and technology to gain protection from her terrible storms, from droughts, from disease. We began to stand apart from her, no longer needing her mercy as we invented ways to farm and store crops, travel to preferred climates, and create medicines. We have traveled outside her atmosphere to the moon, and we intend to one day leave her reach entirely to colonize on planets beyond her gravitational pull. Meanwhile, this new land called Hawaii remains enveloped by our Mother. Hawaii reminds us that our intelligence was born here on Earth, and even if we leave our Mother, her umbilical cord remains evident by the fact that we exist.

Tapping into the energy of the natural world is a sigh of relief for our bodies. It is, of course, partly because we step away from our smartphones and responsibilities, but it is mostly about what we are moving towards—alignment with who we are. Nature offers us connection to the intelligence that lives in everything—humanity, birds, plants, the chair you are sitting on.

The intelligence inside the nut of the palm tree is perfect for the sandy beaches of Maui. The roots of the palm tree grow into a ball shape to better protect itself against tropical hurricanes. The leaves fan out thin and wide to allow wind and rain to pass through easily and cool the tree. The trunks grow tall to access the sunshine above other trees and to store nutrients in case of drought. There is a native intelligence in the atoms of the tree that knows how to thrive in this climate, and this intelligence is encapsulated in the nut. From its birth, the palm tree has everything it needs to thrive.

This same intelligence lives in us. Our bodies know how to thrive. We shiver when we are cold because shivering generates heat. We breathe without thinking (especially when we are asleep!). When we get a cut, we don't wonder how to mend it; we trust our body's innate ability to heal. It is easy to forget that underneath all our thoughts we are connected to the power of our natural intelligence.

After a week or two of sitting in my Colombian backyard, soaking up the rainbow of flora, I noticed a long thick yellowish stalk, almost my height, that stuck out at the edge of the garden. I was a bit annoyed with it as day after day it seemed to do nothing. Unlike everything around it that grew and blossomed and buzzed with life, the stalk stood quiet. It was simply there, a sore thumb in this Monet. After a few days I decided it must be dead. Maybe I could pull it out of the garden and toss it into the woods? I walked up to it, my nose inches away for a thorough inspection.

The wind whistled through the trees and the birds sang out to each other as I stood and gazed at this yellow ski pole in the ground. I stared at it, wanting to know this plant a little bit better, as if I were gathering information to perform a eulogy before uprooting it and throwing it into the woods. It was something I probably wouldn't have done if I weren't alone on private property because I likely looked odd—a woman endlessly staring kissing-distance from a stick. Thankfully, I was alone. Even Ted was inside making love to his fire. I sank into my gaze. There was nothing to defend and nothing to prove, either by me or the plant. It didn't need to be spectacular or vibrant to invite my attention. We were simply standing together, this plant and me.

The air shifted. The weather didn't change, the sun didn't drop behind a cloud, the wind didn't pick up, but the air shifted. Or did I shift? The silence thrummed louder, or was I more aware of it? I leaned into a buzzing layer of aliveness. After a few moments, I noticed that the plant I had thought of as dormant, quiet, and dead was humming. I raised my hand up in front of the stalk as if to give it a high five. Curiously, I felt a tingle in my palm that flowed through my wrist, down my arm, into my chest, and spread throughout my body. My breath deepened.

"*Hello, plant,*" I whispered.

My shoulders relaxed. I hadn't realized how tense they had been. A feeling of unhurriedness washed over me. There was no need to rush through this moment. There was no other moment to get to. Nothing required doing. I wondered if what I felt came from the plant. A knowing settled in my stomach, and again I whispered, this time purposefully, "*Hello, friend.*"

On the coattails of this magical moment clung doubt. This plant was dead. How could it be humming? And then I saw it. On the opposite side of the stalk, which faced away from where I sat every day, was the tiniest green stem, about an inch long. Tucked underneath this little shoot of life was a leaf the size of a raisin. I craned my neck and peered at it, only then noticing that about six inches above this stem was another, a little longer,

70

and at its end was a vanilla-colored bud beginning to bloom, revealing a creamy white flower.

The stalk I had believed was dead was, in fact, alive and thriving. It was moving through its cycle of growth at its own pace, not hurried along by my desire to see what came next. Only when I let go of my expectations, dropped my insistence that the plant delight me because I had become accustomed to nature's vibrant and majestic splendor, did I see its magic. The magic *was* the plant. I felt its pace of life flow through my veins, its unhurriedness in my own body. My heart slowed down and my lungs expanded in rhythm with its energy. Where I typically know nature as something else, something apart from me, in this experience I knew the plant as myself. Subject and object melted into a cosmic soup, and I thought, "*This is what it means to be one with the world.*"

We see ourselves as separate entities. I am not my mom, my brother, or a cat. I am me! If I pinch myself, I feel it. If I pinch the cat, the cat feels it. But this separateness is in many ways only an illusion. It doesn't mean that this notion of separateness isn't valuable or real in other ways. It's simply that the idea of subject and object, me and the plant, isn't the whole truth. I had lived in a world of duality where there were boundaries between us: my bones, my skin, my hair kept me inside myself, as did the plant's roots, stalk, and leaves. But in fact, the only boundary between us was that I *thought* there was a boundary between us. Once I let go of my separateness, we poured into each other.

Not only does natural intelligence live in everything, but it also connects everything. We aren't moving through empty space. Every bit of space and every moment of time are filled with molecules, particles, atoms, and quarks that contain information. Every spot and speck in the entire universe contains intelligence. Everything is connected to everything else through the invisible web of universal intelligence. This cosmic knowing unites All. At this energetic level, there are no true boundaries. In that moment with the plant, I was aware of my connection to the entire world and experienced it within myself.

We have been taught so well how to experience the world with our five senses and this education is so dense that we forget that we are capable of more, that we *are* more. If we are lucky enough to experience something outside of those senses we are at a loss to understand, we do not let it permeate the heaviness of our education. But some of us refuse to toss these moments aside, and this is where the fun begins. This is where we can peer behind the curtain of our learned reality and fumble around the fringed edges of another truth. Who we are is far grander than what we've been taught. Who we are is not limited to our physical experience of life. What is available to us extends beyond the reaches of our five senses. It extends inwards as we plumb the depths of our inner wisdom, and outwards as we experience the intelligence of the world around us. There is nothing beyond our reach, and everything is already in our hands.

MILESTONES

INNER GUIDANCE

- Everything is information.
- There is no empty space in the world. Everything is connected by a cosmic web of universal intelligence.
- Universal intelligence is unbounded by space or time, allowing it to travel and connect freely and instantly.
- We are connected to everything in the universe, with access to all the intelligence of the universe.
- We are the intelligence of the universe. We are built to thrive and everything we need to know is already within us.

DEEPER NAVIGATION

1. Reflect on moments when you feel connected to another—a person, pet, object, or place. This could be a feeling of empathy towards a loved one or the experience of driving and becoming one with your car as it

hugs the road. How do you experience this connection in your mind, heart, and body?

2. Imagine you are connected to the entire universe in every moment, from the smallest molecule to the largest galaxy. Every rock is humming and each tree is standing in service to your desire. The sun, the moon, and the stars are moving in support of your deepest wish. How does this feel? How might this shift your relationship to trust? To fear? To control? To power?

3. For the next week, pay attention to how your intuition speaks to you. Notice that when you meet someone or go somewhere, your gut may offer information that your mind can't explain. Notice when something feels right but you can't explain why. Notice when you make a decision that you can't seem to rationalize. Observe how intelligent you are beyond your five senses.

10

I AM WELLNESS

Danielle and Ted sitting in the Cloud Castle garden (2018)

Tucked into bookshelves and windowsills of the Cloud Castle were all sorts of interesting odds and ends. In addition to the fire-fanning feather, we found a collection of crystals, the Carlos Castaneda book series of

Native American traditions with psychedelics, three small singing bowls, and Tibetan Buddhist flags hanging in the corner of the yoga room. Over the course of our travels these items had become known and even commonplace to us. Ted had carried extremely weathered Tibetan Buddhist flags on his backpack since high school, and I had delved into the world of crystals, carrying a few in a small drawstring pouch inside my backpack for insight, clarity, and a bit of magic everywhere we went. If only my law firm colleagues could see me now! *Trading money for rocks, are you?*

We were surprised to see these items only due to our presumption that Catholic trinkets would take center stage in Colombia. When our new friends came over for dinner, we showed them some of the knickknacks we found, and they clapped their hands in joy.

"Yes, this house is used by the shamans for integration work," Mariana explained.

Ted and I gave each other a quizzical look, as we had never heard anything about shamans here. What had we stumbled into? "What kind of integration work?" I asked.

Mariana fussed with her scrubs. She was a doctor by day and an alternative medicine student by night, focusing on Chinese and Ayurvedic traditions as well as those offered by local plants. "Well, they work with tourists, mostly veterans who are seeking psychedelic treatment and come down through the Heroic Hearts Project. You two are living in a rural town and shamans are part of our culture. They've been here forever, guiding the town in ritual ceremonies as called upon either by our calendar or by request of a townsperson."

I couldn't believe my luck to have parachuted into this magical world. *Thanks crystals!* I wanted to know everything and asked Mariana to continue.

"Depending on the time of year, we gather in ceremony for different purposes and with different plant teachers. Every generation joins the ceremony. It's not like up north where these things are subversive or even recreational. This is the glue that holds the town together. This is how we pray together, grow together, and grieve together. For instance, if someone lost a parent or a child, they could ask the shamans to hold a ceremony to support them, and we would all come together to do that."

I noticed that one of our neighbors had an incredibly large teepee on the property and asked Mariana if that property was also used for ceremonies.

"Oh, that's the shamans' house," she said as she waved out the window. "That's where they live with their wives and children. Right now, they are in Australia sharing rituals with some Australian shamans, so that's why this house is empty. They aren't here to do any ceremonial work with tourists, so the property is all yours."

I immediately pictured white people retching all over this house as they moved through the discomfort that is often a part of such sacred plant ceremonies. I could feel the density of their emotional upheaval.

"Actually, next week is when we do our San Pedro ceremony. You are both welcome to join us. We would love to have you." Mariana remarked.

"Yes!" I cried in glee. What a unique opportunity! Ted and I had a fair amount of experience with entheogens (psychoactive substances, especially those derived from plants like psilocybin or ayahuasca) but had never tried San Pedro and had never sat for a traditional ceremony with a native shaman.

Our other friend, a veteran ex-pat named David, piped up, "Actually, I don't think it will be San Pedro since our shamans are gone."

My heart sank at the thought of missing out, but then Mariana corrected herself. "Right, our visiting shaman is from the Lakota tribe in Mexico, so he will be offering peyote, the grandfather cactus from his tradition. That's great because we will all be in the same boat together. None of us know what this ceremony will be like!"

Ted bounced up from his seat with excitement. "Okay, great, what do we need to know to prepare?"

Mariana and David laughed, both offering the other the invitation to answer his question. Mariana took the lead, as her partner was one of Santa Elena's shamans and she was intimately knowledgeable about the tradition. "First of all, Danielle, you must know that it is impossible for you to join our ceremony if you are on your cycle. I'm sorry to say but it's a strict requirement. The menstrual cycle disrupts the flow of energy from the plant and it also makes you more susceptible to absorbing other people's energies, which you don't want to do." I wasn't going to be on my period and was quite relieved.

"Okay, what else to know? Well, here is the diet that we follow before ceremonies. It's not that strict, don't worry. Try not to eat sugar, dairy, pork, or anything spicy for the two days leading up to the ceremony. Also don't engage with any other plant teachers during this time," she said as she pointed over to the mason jar of cannabis oil that David carried everywhere.

"Wear something comfortable as it will be a long night, but no pajamas. Bring a candle, some fruit, and plenty of water. And bring as many pillows and blankets as you can. There's never too many."

And that was it. Our marching orders barely pierced the shroud of mystery cloaking this experience.

Then David explained to us that we needed to go to the town pharmacy sometime that week to pay for our tickets. This totally took me by surprise. Tickets? Pharmacy? It was so out in the open here and a part of the community that the transactional aspect of purchasing our tickets for the medicine was an everyday affair that we could handle while grabbing a bottle of aspirin.

The pharmacy was in the middle of town, which was nothing more than a small cul-de-sac on the road leading down the mountain from our house. There was a grocery store, a coffee shop, a few restaurants, an ice cream shop, a lumber store (everyone needed firewood), and the pharmacy. If you're picturing the bright fluorescent lights shining above the huge white shelves of a Walgreens, try again. This was a chicken-coop sized hut with a screen door that opened to standing room for about two patrons. When we went inside, Ted showed the clerk the note that Mariana wrote for us explaining what we wanted. My insides squirmed, trained to expect a side eye glance or judgment. But no, the clerk took our note and nodded up and down. Business as usual. He deposited our 100,000 pesos ($33 USD) into the shaman's account and handed over a printed receipt for us to present at the ceremony as proof of payment.

When the evening of the ceremony came, Ted and I gathered mats, pillows, blankets, water, fruit, a candle each, and put on comfortable clothing. With the sun hanging low at about 7:30, David picked us up in his car—a glorified golf cart—and drove us about twenty minutes to the property where we'd spend the next twelve hours uncoiling ourselves.

It was dark when we pulled off a very small road onto a narrow dirt drive. There was one large structure standing in the middle of the woods.

A smiling woman greeted us at the door and opened her hand to see our receipts, which we presented gratefully. She waved us into the building, which was one huge empty room with a bamboo ceiling and a bathroom. We followed David to a corner of the room and lined our mats and blankets against the wall. I gazed around the room to get my bearings and noticed that everyone seemed to find a space to settle into along the walls of the room, creating a big circle around an empty chair in the middle, presumably for the shaman. Someone was stoking a fire in the fireplace at one end of the room, sending the familiar scent of burning pine and eucalyptus wafting through the air.

"We're lucky to get space against the wall," David whispered to me. "You aren't allowed to lay down or go to sleep the entire night, so it's nice to have something to lean your back against."

Oh my god. Somehow the rigors of what a traditional, indigenous ceremony entailed had escaped my mind. My entire experience of psychedelics was one of freedom—freedom to roam, freedom to get cozy under a blanket, freedom to listen to music, freedom to open the fridge and get lost inside a carton of juice. I realized that I was submitting myself to an experience where I gave full rein to someone else. Suddenly I was transported back to synagogue as a child, sitting in the pews with my family during services and following the directives of the rabbi to stand up, sit down, flip to page whatever and read along with the congregation, stand up, sit down again. How bored I was! I had no idea why I was standing up and sitting down or what the Hebrew I was singing even meant. Was I about to slide into the pews of the Lakota tradition?

The room slowly filled with women, children, uncles, and grandmothers. Every member of the community was there, greeting each other, singing, the children dancing joyously around the room. They had all put on something nice over their sweatpants to show respect for the occasion, whether a simple dress, a beaded belt, or a colorful headband. The room grew so crowded that a direct line of sight to the fire was impossible, so we angled ourselves as best we could without turning our backs on anyone.

After a few hours the shaman, called the Marakame in his tradition, came inside and settled into his chair. Dressed in a white shirt and pants with red embroidery on the trim and birds sewn down the back, he exuded mysticism. Feathers poked out of the weaves in his white-and-tan sombrero that sat atop a faded blue baseball cap turned sideways. A local woman from the community explained how the Marakame's ceremony would be conducted. Everything was in Spanish, and not even our Colombian friends were quite sure of what was going on. Ted spoke enough Spanish to get the gist and whispered a translation to me. The woman came around the room with pieces of chocolate and cookies and told us to take a piece of each and put it in two cups. She came around again and said a blessing over each of us with a wave of a feather and copal, a natural incense made of tree resin used for ceremonial purposes as far back as the Mayans.

The participants passed around a tobacco paste they dipped into with their pinkies and a coca powder that they spooned into their cheeks for energy through the night. David explained that the tobacco paste helps release the coca alkaloids for easier and faster digestion. I skipped it as I've never smoked a cigarette in my life and didn't think this was the optimal moment to try two new substances.

All the peyote newbies were to receive a special blessing from the Marakame. Ted and I got up from our cozy blankets and formed a line with the others. One by one, we kneeled at the feet of this mystic who traced the pointy end of his feather through the peyote powder and said a prayer while he touched it to our cheeks, our wrists, to a piece of corn, and offered a tiny bit into a bowl.

After everyone was seated, it was explained that the peyote would be passed around to us and the Marakame would sing five songs through the night until sunrise. Then came the rules. No sleeping. No lying down. No talking. No eating. The same woman came around with a giant jar of finely ground peyote and dosed out a healthy tablespoon of a light sandy brown powder into each person's cupped hand. Watching those who went before me, I dumped the medicine into my mouth followed by a giant swig of water to gulp it down. There's no way around how acrid it tasted. My mouth puckered and I tried not to let my facial expression betray me. Everyone else seemed to have swallowed sugar. In perfect timing, the woman explained where she put the puke buckets in case the medicine invited us to purge. That much I could understand without translation. Then the Marakame's helpers waved more copal around the room.

The room fell dark but for the glow of the fire. The Marakame and a few others started beating drums to the rhythm of the medicine. In a gentle, rumbling voice, the Marakame sang songs giving praise to the peyote plant, the fire, and the water. Ted whispered a few of the words he understood, something about a bear and a fox. I couldn't follow along and my head grew heavy and uncomfortable. It seemed ridiculous that my broomstick of a neck was expected to hold up my giant head all by itself. I was granted reprieve from the discomfort in my neck when my stomach started churning. Shifting focus to the songs and humming along helped enormously. Meanwhile, the babies slept soundly as the room grew warm and full, voices sharing in joyful prayer to the melody of a guitar that had joined the drum. I drifted between praying not to puke and praying for spiritual enlightenment.

I grappled with all the rules of this traditional ceremony. When I was growing up, rules were good because they offered guidance to navigate the world. I fell in love with rules, wanting to master them and leverage them. They were my path to success. By the time I quit my law firm, rules had transformed into shackles. Rules were constraining, restrictive, oppressive, meant to brainwash and civilize the masses. Rules were directives disguised in garments of truth. I craved freedom and psychedelics offered that freedom, liberating me from stories and obligations. Nancy Reagan would have been so disappointed; I had been such a good D.A.R.E. kid my entire life (until I passed the bar exam). Nothing about this ceremony pointed towards that freedom and I was primed to resent all its rules.

But in perfect universal fashion, the traditions of the Marakame and the ceremony he created offered a real freedom I hadn't yet known. The rules of the ceremony were not meant to limit, but to create. They were not good or bad; they were boundaries that formed a space in which my experience could unfold. They didn't tell me what kind of experience I must have or what I should feel or what I needed to learn. The rules required my attention to be in this room, to be with these people, to be with the songs, and to be with myself. All the wisdom showed up in the space between the distractions my mind and body craved.

After spending months purposefully and vigorously eschewing rules, the ceremony showed me how I was still attached to them. I was stuck in a paradigm in which rules were either good or bad. It took as much energy to follow them as it took to resist them. Either way, they still defined my life. A rule to not live by rules is still, quite annoyingly, a rule. It was like declaring I no longer wanted to look at the front of my hand and turning it around to look at the back. I wasn't really looking at something new; it was still the shape of my hand. I relaxed into a space where the good versus bad paradigm was irrelevant. The purpose of rules became clear—to create shape. A hand, a ceremony, a life.

Time was evanescent. I only remembered time when I was preoccupied by the discomfort of my body, measuring its passage by how often the nausea consumed me. Otherwise, I sank deeply into a world within my imagination. With closed eyes, beautiful neon images flickered by in the style of Lite-Brite, a toy from my childhood in which you poked colored pegs into a backlit screen, creating glowing designs. My thoughts quieted and disappeared until I was watching a movie of brightly colored shapes. Without thought, there was no coherent story line. The images were abstract and moved with the songs. Every so often I'd return to thoughts and wonder what I had seen, giving the shapes meaning they otherwise lacked.

I realized some of the images I saw were scary—monsters, dragons, deep dark woods that no light could pierce. But in the moment I saw them, they weren't scary. They were simply shapes and colors. They held no qualities at all, and I held no judgment of them. There was no perspective through which to understand, to compartmentalize, to say, "Ah, this is this and that is that." There was no framework—or rules—to delineate what was scary, or even what was interesting. The whole idea of fear became funny; I smiled to myself in the darkness. The rules that told me what scary was had gone, poof, disappeared.

I loved it. Then I wondered, *Does this apply to happiness, too?* Without a framework, would everything feel like nothing?

"It's a choice," I heard a Voice say. It wasn't my Voice this time, but the deep gravelly voice of a wizened old man. He said, "You are the ground upon which you build the carnival."

All of this was quite clear, obvious under the tutelage of the medicine. The only tricky part was listening to the lesson while my body threw a temper tantrum. Peyote reminded me that there was something deeper underneath my fascination with rules for life. Yes, my rules for fear and joy create carnival rides: the joy of a merry-go-round and the fear of a house of mirrors, but these frameworks are all negotiable. There are the stretching and molding of my playdough. Peyote pointed me to look underneath these rides to something constant and unyielding: the ground. We can visit the carnival on Tuesday and find scary roller coasters and then when we arrive on Saturday it's full of tunnels of love, but no matter what rides we find, they are all supported by the ground. The ground can hold all the ups and downs of life.

Peyote was inviting me to notice not just my ability to create, but the fundamental power that supports creation. We are the ground that supports all our life experience. This ground is our foundational, natural state before we layer on experience. This ground is wellness. *We are wellness.* I don't mean physical, mental, or emotional wellness. Our wellness is our ability to experience anything and everything life brings—all the rides of life. Wellness doesn't mean we don't encounter illness of the body or mind, but that those are our *experiences* and not who we are. There is nothing wrong with us if we endure cancer or PTSD, heartbreak or Alzheimer's. These experiences often influence the carnival rides we build, but they don't change the fact that they are built on solid ground.

Underneath our illness is our wellness. It allows us to experience every single expression of what's possible. Of course we can, otherwise we would be such fragile creatures. If we couldn't handle a confusing tilt-a-whirl or the stress of bumper cars, then we wouldn't be able to handle the breadth of human experience. We can. It's evident when we look at how each and every person across the globe experiences a unique life. Each is different from the next. And that's just the point: we are built for all of it.

Our capacity for all life experience is constant and unyielding. When we doubt our wellness, we are simply caught up in whatever carnival ride we built for ourselves and can't feel the ground beneath our feet. But the carnival ride will end—they all do—and we will have more opportunities to remember our wellness. This happens to me all the time. I'll be wound up in fear and doubt about a situation, like wondering if I could afford my mortgage payment after a month of unpaid client invoices. But as days, weeks, and months go by, I look back and realize at some point I got off the roller coaster and settled into wellness. I often don't even realize when it happens because wellness is my default state. Rather, I notice the ups and downs of life—when I am *not* settled into my wellness. These moments compel my attention. Sooner or later, the carnival ride is over and I rarely even acknowledge that I'm no longer stuck on the ride.

The woman came around with the jar of peyote twice more over the next few hours and waved more copal around the room to invite good energy. The dense pungent fog urged me to step outside for some fresh air. An outdoor bonfire burned, located conveniently near a puke bucket, and I felt instant relief. I felt like I had been tortured into enlightenment. I was worn out, uncomfortable, confused, and alone for most of the night. The only comfort came by surrendering to the plant, letting it guide me to dimensions where my physicality was irrelevant. Not long after I stepped outside, everyone came out for a mid-ceremony tobacco ritual that involved blowing cigar smoke into the bonfire. I had no idea whether it was midnight or almost dawn. We went back inside and I shamefully fell asleep for ten minutes or an hour, who's to say. When Ted gently nudged me, the woman was coming around with a morning dose of medicine, only a teaspoon this time, the hair of the dog. I couldn't believe it. I politely declined while Ted gleefully accepted.

Morning rays filtered through the windows and people started milling around, grabbing handfuls of fruit from a giant bucket near the Marakame to take back to their families. A breakfast brew was passed around and I took a big gulp before realizing it was Chicha, a traditional Colombian drink of fermented corn, sugar, and various herbs. Allegedly a low alcoholic content, the taste told me otherwise. I saw another drink being passed among the women that looked more like a sweet juice, but I had no energy to get up and try it. David later explained to me that it is called *caguana*, a brew made of yucca starch, pineapple, and panela (Colombian sugar). The yucca starch gives it a texture designed to resemble embryonic fluid as a part of its prayer for bringing sweetness and purifying energy to women.

We left on the edge of politeness, as I was dying to eat something hot and chewy and lie down horizontally. I thought it was past noon by the time we left, but it was barely 7a.m. David drove us to his favorite fried potato guy and to a bakery to grab some food that we wolfed down, mercilessly getting crumbs all over his car. With my immediate physical needs met, I sank into the experience I had been through. What surfaced was, *what a ride!*

MILESTONES

INNER GUIDANCE

∂ We imbue life with meaning based on our rules or frameworks. These tell us what is scary or exciting, good or bad, important or inconsequential.

∂ These frameworks shape our experiences—our "carnival rides."

∂ Each ride is built on the ground of *wellness*, which is our natural state.

∂ Our wellness allows us to experience all the ups and downs of life.

∂ Everyone is riding on their own, uniquely built carnival rides, but everyone's carnival is built upon this same ground.

DEEPER NAVIGATION

1. What carnival ride are you on right now? Notice any moments when the ride stops and you settle into wellness. This could be a day, an hour, or a single breath.

2. Reflect on your life and when your innate wellness shows up. Look for patterns here, as they offer insight to tap into your wellness any time.

3. Play with the perspective of innate wellness and view others through that lens. Take note of those whom you may consider to be physically or mentally unwell. At some point during the day, they are likely to settle into wellness. Notice that this space is always within them.

11

I AM MAGIC

Temple at Burning Man (2018)

The wooden beams wrap around the temple in an upward spiral, creating a funnel that looks like the cover of Dr. Seuss's *Oh, the Places You'll Go.* The prayers of those inside are pushed skywards through this spiritual canal to be birthed anew in the wide-open desert on the other side. This barren land is the bottom of an ancient lake, and the sand is actually dust. It is desolate, dry, and brown until it boldly erupts into a spotless blue sky. No trees, no cacti, no splotch of shrubbery—no life can be sustained here. Except the place itself is alive. The energy of this desert is buzzing with aliveness.

The temple is resurrected for a week each summer for the celebration of Burning Man. It may not look the same each year, but its annual appearance summons 80,000 people and their prayers, burdens, hopes, blessings, and tears. Is Burning Man a celebration? Sure, if you're celebrating. It's whatever you want it to be. It's a celebration, a festival, a mobile and temporary civilization, a ritual, a revolution, an energy vortex, and an opportunity to remember who you are.

Much of the city that gets erected is built as bliss bait, the many offerings that promise a good time—the sound stages for sunrise DJ sets, the art installations casting LED lights across the stars, the orgy dome, and the costume camps. But the temple stands apart from the raucousness. A quick ride on my bicycle away from the lights and sounds and I arrive at this quiet, stoic place. I feel the energy shift as I get off my bike and park it next to a clump of bikes about twenty feet from the temple. My heart slows and my skin prickles as I approach the holy spiral.

The architecture of the beams allows every open space to serve as an entrance. It is completely in flow, allowing energy in from any perspective and energy out through one skyward spout.

A woman with enormous, crinkly hair dressed in black boots, a ripped desert skirt, and a black top kneels in front of me at the foot of the temple, playing an accordion and singing what sounds like a Sanskrit meditative chant. I sit down in the dust to listen. A large crowd of souls is drawn to her music. When her song ends, I stand up and dust off my legs, more out of habit than in any genuine effort to be clean. I meander into the temple, observing people in all states of prayer. There are no pews to sit on. People wander around the cavernous space doing and saying and praying however they like.

I needed a transformative experience here. I had been to plenty of synagogues, but my experience with them was mostly form over function, a recitation of prayers without much spiritual animation behind them. When I'd look around the room at the congregants, they mostly seemed obedient and respectful. No one looked to be in the throes of spiritual rapture, fully experiencing the divine. But in the middle of the desert inside this wooden temple, I felt God communing with everyone around me, a silk scarf sliding between us and wrapping around us.

Some meditated alone in a quiet corner while others sat melded together deep in embrace. Some cried silently while others wailed with the commitment of a *muaddin* (the caller to prayer). There was no wrong way to dive within and bring your depths to the surface. No right way to wring out your insides. Emotions hung heavy in the air, creating wakes and currents as I walked through and between people. I had never experienced something like this before, and I expected something extraordinary, something transformative amidst this sea of passionately disrobing hearts.

If I had learned anything from my experiences up to this point, it was to surrender my mind, open my heart, and let it all pour in. I waited for the energy to catch me like a surfer catching a wave and take me somewhere glorious. I waited. I breathed. I observed. I waited more. I felt nothing.

Unsure of what to do next, I got up and walked around, reading some of the letters and prayers people tucked inside the temple to burn on the last night when the structure would be set aflame. Maybe reading other people's most intimate words would spark something? It didn't. My soul did not feel amplified, my heart did not wring with emotion like a wet rag. I felt so even, almost flat. While it was an experience I hadn't expected, it was not what I was looking for. I was bummed. I was ready to dive headfirst into all this energy and let it carry me on a current of its own making, but here I was standing solidly on my feet and scratching my head.

I sighed and resigned myself to this being enough for now and walked towards the outside of the temple. At the temple's edge I noticed a man wedging a vibrantly painted canvas, with swirls of red, orange, and yellow overlaid with black writing, into the space between two beams. I tapped him on the shoulder and told him, "I like your painting. It's beautiful."

"Thanks." He turned to look at me. He was tall and lean, with short, cropped hair and sad eyes. "It's for my brother. He died last year."

My hand reached for his arm. "I'm sorry."

At my touch he crumpled into a heap, crying into my neck. Big wet tears streamed down my shoulders, his chest heaving in short raspy breaths. A minute went by, two minutes went by as we held each other. He stopped crying enough to speak choppy words between gasps for air.

"I have been trying not to feel the pain of his death," he said. I nodded. "I feel it now," he whispered.

I nodded again. I was secretly happy to spark such an emotional upheaval, even if it wasn't mine. We are always both giver and receiver, and although I didn't know it then, he had offered me exactly what I'd been looking for. Still holding his arms, I asked, "How does it feel?"

He winced at my question. It's one thing to let down the floodgates that are holding back feelings and another to look directly at what is pouring in.

He blurted, "It hurts so bad," before collapsing into a puddle, my shoulder drenched in the desert sun. Silent, I let him continue to cry, to feel the pain, to feel whatever he needed to feel. We stayed that way for a while, through the ebb and flow of a good cry. Long wails turned to short sniffles, a reprieve of a few breaths, and back to messy sobs. I thought about how hard we try to cut ourselves off from our feelings. How we've been taught to be strong, which somehow means to have a stiff upper lip. How we busy ourselves in order to move on, but we are only being distracted and disconnected. Underneath all this learning is what we *know*. In the center of all our pain is a raw nerve and to touch it is to be alive.

After a while I gently squeezed his arms and he looked up at me, desperation filled his eyes, as if asking me what to do with his feelings now. He had been afraid of them for so long.

I smiled and started to breathe, modeling something for him to follow. Together we slowly inhaled peace through our noses, slowly filling ourselves with peace from our bellies up through the crown of our heads. I had no idea if this was a real breathing exercise, but it came rolling out of me before doubt over my ineptness could stop it.

Now calmer, he told me how thankful he was to feel, even though it hurt. His chin wobbled. His eyes fluttered and he heaved a breath. "I love him so much. I miss him so much." He started crying again. This time he tried to talk through syncopated sobs, but I couldn't understand much of the muffled noises coming from my shoulder.

It went on like this for a bit, talking about feeling, feeling the feeling, and crying out the feeling. He told me his brother passed away the previous year and that he had committed suicide. Suddenly I felt a rush up my spine. Something reached into me like smoke curling its way into my body. It needed me to share something this man already knew but didn't yet believe. I was scared to say the words because they came from somewhere unfamiliar to me, but I knew my fear shouldn't stop this moment. Somehow it was clear that this sensation came from the crossed-over brother, and my fear had no role to play in this conversation between family members.

"Your brother wants you to know that he went home." I looked at this man and his eyes caught me squarely in my soul. A fish hooked on the line, I had to continue. "He is so happy now. He wants you to know that. He is happy. He did the right thing for himself."

Nodding, his mouth quivered and his eyes crinkled. "I know," he said, bobbing his head up and down. "He had so many demons. He took care of everyone else, but he couldn't take care of himself."

More tingling in my spine, urgent now. I said, "But he did take care of himself in the end. He needed to go home. He's *so happy* now and he wants you to know," I repeated, the intensity of the brother's joy reverberating through me, my own tears starting to flow.

"I wish I could have . . . I'm his big brother!" Guilt in his eyes, he looked at me with sadness and confusion, but also with love. He felt accountable for his brother's suicide.

"You aren't responsible for anyone's choices but your own." I offered. Again, these weren't my words. The sentiments were coming directly from the other side of the cosmic veil. "You are his brother. He loves you. He went home because he wanted to love himself, too." My eyes teared up as I felt his brother's easy, effortless love. Any self-doubt, shame, and disappointment that clung to his physical experience of life was gone, as easy as wiping crumbs off a sweater. He shone as a pure bright light. Nothing could dim his spirit in this realm, and despite his ethereal nature, his presence in the temple was solid. Through my voice, he blessed his brother, wishing for him to brush off his guilt so that he could embrace the love waiting underneath.

The man nodded in agreement. A flicker of doubt passed through my mind as I considered whether to stop dancing around it and plainly tell him that I was communicating with his brother. I could hardly believe it myself. If the experience wasn't so visceral, so urgent, I might have denied it and went on as though I had thought of these words. But this experience was no match for my doubt, a doubt that felt so puny in the face of cosmic intelligence. It only had the power to tickle my mind for an instant before the words tumbled out of my mouth, "Your brother is with us. Do you know that?"

"I hear him talk to me sometimes." As he said it, he seemed unsure in the same way that I was unsure. Communicating with the dead was not an experience I had before. I had practiced and played with energy and consciousness plenty of times through various modalities like reiki, telepathy, synchronicity, and visualization, and it had been wildly fun and many times successful, but only with "real" people. This crossed into very new territory. I had never thought about communicating with the dead. That sounded too far-fetched even for me. Mediums seemed like charlatans for the most part, and those who had gained the reputation of legitimacy seemed more mystical than I could ever hope to be. I was working with energy beyond my five senses, but only as far as I could validate it. How could I prove I was talking to this guy's brother? I couldn't, and so doubt came pouring in.

What I did know was that I felt energy. It was buzzing through my body in waves, with these thoughts coming from somewhere else and self-identifying as this man's brother. Electricity coursed through my veins and flowed through my fingers and toes, my head, my stomach. I hugged this tall man in front of me and held him heart to heart. The electricity flowing through me formed a white mist, and I directed it to flow out through my hands and into his back where my hands met his skin. In my mind's eye, I watched this mist move through his back, his spine, his diaphragm; he took a huge breath and hugged me tighter. The mist continued, spreading through his chest and limbs and hands, cascading out of his palms and pouring back into my body.

The energy circuit was complete. He stepped back and looked at me, "I feel that."

He straightened up a bit, his demeanor slow and stable. This energy grounded him. "This is how I feel when I'm at peace with what happened to my brother."

Of course, the energy running through me *was* peace. For me it felt alive, electric, thrumming with potential. For this man, he felt peace. "My brother must feel peace, since I'm feeling him." He concluded.

His words almost knocked me over like an ocean wave. He had resonated with his own inner wisdom on a deeper level than I could offer with my own words of comfort. He experienced truth on a level our minds can't touch with doubt. Grounded deeply in his knowing, he was free to release the pain, the shame, and the guilt. They no longer held any power, held no sway over his perspective. The energy of peace was compelling in its completeness.

I knew nothing of his brother's story, which wasn't relevant, so I didn't ask. The details seemed like a distraction from the alchemy that we were experiencing. But something nagged at me. "What's your brother's name?" I asked.

"Dan. Daniel," he responded.

I smiled and wiped a tear running down my cheek. "My name is Danielle."

He cocked his head to the side, his mouth agape, words caught in his throat. "Daniel. Danielle. Really?" He laughed and it turned into the beginnings of a sob. "That's magic. How does that happen?"

Chuckling, I threw my palms in the air and said, "I don't know. It's the Universe."

A cry stuck in his throat and he nodded, smiling through the tears. "It's amazing."

We hugged again, finding calm strength in each other's breath. The world rushed back in. I noticed the dust blowing everywhere, the heat of the sun beating down, other people's voices singing and chatting. Out of the corner of my eye I saw a friend I had biked here with waving me over. It was time to go. I released my new friend from my embrace, rubbed his arms gently, and asked if he would be okay when I left. He said yes and thanked me for being in this moment with him.

There isn't enough vitality to the word grateful, but if you can imagine pouring some cold water on it to wake it up and stretch it open like a clay pinch pot, that is how I felt walking away from the Temple. Awake, open, and stretched. It was more than I could have ever expected. It moved me beyond what I thought possible, a place that seemed too far out on the cosmic field for an attorney. Thankfully, there was no way my mind could convince me to disown this experience and it forced my perspective to expand. By this point I had forged a strong connection to my own energy and could even share this connection with other people, even plants! But I had never considered playing with universal intelligence this way. Was there an end to the ways we could communicate with, participate with, and interact with universal intelligence? How much power to access this intelligence did I have? Obviously more than I had ever imagined.

In time, my mind caught up and found a way to fit what happened in the temple into a framework that I could accept. I was so adamantly stubborn in what I experienced that my brain had to find a way to "make it work" (*a la* Tim Gunn of *Project Runway*). It's amazing that if I tell my mind what it needs to do, it will accommodate. It's in charge of the picture, but I'm in charge of the frame.

I was so glad I hadn't formed a specific intention at the temple for how I wanted my experience to unfold. I would never have asked for this. This was a peek behind the illusive curtain of duality in a way that collapsed all separateness. Life from death. Me from another. The magic was in allowing my state of mind to relax into Oneness, to surrender my separateness from everything else, whether it is a plant or the formless spirit of a man. Magic dances in the place where there is no space between us.

While channeling the messages of a dead brother has a certain sensational appeal, it's not the point. People are intoxicated by the notion of superpowers like seeing the future, healing the sick, and communing with the dead. Extraordinary abilities are exotic and powerful. Why wouldn't we want them? But if they are the goal, then you're missing their true power. They are tools, like sight, hearing, smell, taste, and touch. What these tools offer us is access to a fuller, broader experience of life. They are tools to access more planes of consciousness and more dimensions of being human. They are tools that help us uncage ourselves from the limited experience we are taught is "reality" to roam freely in any direction we want to go.

This experience gifted me a deeper relationship with empathy. While the man in front of me crumpled to tears, I held my center still. I felt his sadness, his tears licked my insides, but I remained at peace. My calm was undisturbed. I didn't have to give it up to empathize with his sadness. I didn't need to fall to pieces to honor his feelings. After that day at the temple, it became much easier to turn on the power of empathy. It offers such beautiful insight into another person's world, without needing to sacrifice anything of my own.

But that's not the power of empathy that I most treasure. If I have the power to resonate with someone else's energy, they can resonate with mine. By *not* sacrificing my calm, I offer an invitation to anyone around me to empathize with me and find peace within themselves. Who is served if we dim our own light to match the dimness of others? No one. Who is served when we offer our light to the world? Everyone.

That afternoon at the temple blew me away. *Of course,* this magical moment came only when I surrendered any expectations of it. *Of course,* it showed up more powerfully than I could ever have imagined if I had set a specific goal. Hadn't I learned all of this already? I saw how my inner being knew what I wanted more than my mind ever could, and how it directed my most efficient path to experience it. It trotted me around the temple long enough to tire me out and let go of my "need" for a transformative experience. As soon as I surrendered my mind and headed out of the temple, the magical moment fell into my lap. As soon as I had no requirements or parameters for what it should look like, there were no limits to what it could look like. It showed me wisdom, connection, empathy, and magic across the planes of existence. It showed me how powerful humans are and what is available to us.

MILESTONES

INNER GUIDANCE

> Universal intelligence knows no bounds. It is unbounded by space, time, and physicality. We have the innate power and ability to access this universal intelligence in more ways than we could ever imagine.
> When we let go of a specific goal, we make room for the universe to show us more than we could have asked for.

- When we surrender our minds and open our hearts, we make room for magic. Lean into the magic and more magic will follow.
- Empathy, or clairsentience, is when we clearly can feel the world of another. We do not need to sacrifice how we feel to do this.
- When we hold onto our center, we offer a much greater gift than if we plummet into another's sadness. When we hold onto our inner calm, we extend an invitation for others to empathize with us. We offer them an opportunity to feel what we feel and find calm within themselves.

DEEPER NAVIGATION

1. Reflect on a moment where you learned something was possible. For example, it could be learning as a child that water turns to ice, or that you could salsa dance. How did it feel? Did you navigate any self-doubt?
2. Moments of serendipity tend to happen when we have let go of needing an experience to be a certain way. These moments can catapult us past our goals to places we couldn't have imagined. Write down a goal you have—big or small. Then write how you would feel when you reach your goal. How would your life change? Really tap into your heart and your imagination here. This is a time to slow down and be with your *why*. Once you're finished, focus on your vision and the feelings that come with it, and drop the goal. Notice the space you've opened up to allow your vision to be birthed.
3. Notice moments where life gives you exactly what you want—big and small. No need to do anything about it but notice how much magic exists in the world.

PART III

EXPANSION

A very little key will open a very heavy door.

—CHARLES DICKENS

12

I AM COMMITTED

Danielle in Santa Monica, California (2018)

I sat outside at a trendy café in Santa Monica, sipping a coffee and soaking up the sunshine, my favorite pastime. Ted and I had decided to try out California living for a month to see what all the fuss was about. East Coasters are always dreaming of California. Its allure was instilled in me through the beautiful paintings hung throughout my childhood home of San Francisco's Russian Hill and the rocky SoCal coastline dotted with purple bougainvillea.

Back in my home country, where I spoke the language and could navigate the culture, my body exhaled. I welcomed the easy "newness" of California. My foot bopped along to the indie music playing over the outdoor speaker as I sipped my overpriced lavender-scented latte. In the U.S. for the first time in a long time, I wondered if I'd return to my old ways. Would my old persona creep back in if I spent enough time in the land of the stars and stripes? Doubt started to sneak its way into the beautiful afternoon, unfurling like a dense fog.

Shit, I wondered mid-coffee sip. *Is this all bullshit?*

Even though I knew I'd had incredible experiences that expanded my understanding of who I was and the nature of reality, I couldn't taste them or touch them anymore. They felt far away, an ethereal dream that slid through my grasp. Did any of it really happen? I *thought* I had traded my external labels for internal wisdom. But sitting here at this café, I felt the all-too familiar vibe of my old stories closing in on me. *I should have worn makeup today. What do people think of me having a coffee in yoga pants on a weekday morning? I should have brought my laptop so I could look productive.* Now that I was stateside, I realized I had left the stability of my newly formed reality across the ocean. I felt wobbly, craving the validation of these strangers in bike shorts eating gluten-free quiche. Were all the insights I had collected another mirage of self-identity?

Isn't it obvious that I should know who I am? I thought I did before I ever asked the question! I thought I knew who I was before I quit my job and packed up my Washington D.C. apartment. At least I knew what I was getting dressed for in the morning and where I was going when I got off the metro. I had a *purpose*, even if it was one I didn't like. All this globetrotting pointed me in a completely different direction. But here at this coffee shop my doubts held me captive, and my compass spun wildly trying to locate true north. I dangled between two realities. It was troubling that I couldn't pin myself down. *Who was I?* Who would be better at answering this question than I was?

Oh god, I thought. Was I sitting here in the California sunshine having *another* identity crisis? Was quitting my legal career to find out who I am merely the telltale sign of a quarter-life meltdown? Was I being fooled, brainwashed by the trip of self-realization? I didn't feel realized, actualized, understood, or powerful. I felt confused. *What have I done?* I thought, as I shook my head and tried not to cry. Had I made a huge mistake to leave my life in D.C.? My mind was a churning sea. I looked for a lifeline out of the storm, but every thought was a wave slapping me down.

The sidewalk started spinning under my feet. Was I getting brain-addled by all this golden sun? East Coasters weren't built for this much light. Doubt's darkness swallowed me whole. The once visceral connection I had to my new reality felt too ethereal to anchor me as I fell into the abyss of insecurity. My mind offered me a proposition, "Prove these new insights about yourself are true and I'll leave you alone. If you resolve the doubt, I'll have to let you move on."

Argh. I knew this was a trick. I knew it because of how reasonable it sounded. Nothing about the journey of self-discovery is reasonable. My mind demanded proof, evidence, something concrete. I didn't have any of those things, and it knew I didn't. I didn't come away from these experiences with a button or a T-shirt to show for it. There were only my experiences, whose truth lived in the memory of my heart. Was this good enough for my mind, which had a very clever way of using doubt to shroud my faith? What was once solid and clear felt hazy and shapeless. I knew I was experiencing shaking my own water bottle and clouding it with the sand of my thoughts, but I couldn't sort out how to set it down.

What kind of proof could I offer? My mind was such a terrific trickster. It backed me into a corner and made me want to throw my hands up and say, "You win," pack up my bags, and head back to D.C. to see if I could pick up where I left off.

But I couldn't. I couldn't surrender. There was no way I was going back to D.C. or interviewing at law firms to put on a blazer and clack away at a computer. I took a deep breath and noticed the tension in my body. My mind pulled at me, playing tug of war, but there was something on the other end of the rope holding fast against the pull of doubt. Some deeper, silent force, gentle but insistent. It didn't goad me into playing any games or require any proof, but it was also never going to let go.

"*Keep going,*" my Voice whispered.

Ah, there you are. Right.

If I couldn't go backwards, I must go forwards. I didn't know what that looked like, but I knew it was my direction. True north. I exhaled relief, and the tension left my body. I no longer needed to engage in my mind's tug of war. I didn't need to tackle doubt to the ground and pummel it out of existence to move forward. I didn't need to jump through any hoops or solve any puzzles or expend any effort on these thoughts of doubt at all. I could move forward *with doubt*.

Having taken the "red pill" when I quit the law firm wasn't about falling down the rabbit hole of self-discovery, but about a *commitment* to the journey. I couldn't un-take the red pill. I was never promised a journey free of doubt, anxiety, stress, or confusion. What the red pill promised was that this calm clear space of inner wisdom would never leave me. It *was* me. This space housed my Voice. My work was to remember to point my attention in the direction of this beacon. Doubt might flicker around the edges, but it was no match for the brilliance of my inner lighthouse.

The question, *Who am I?* was my mind's trick. Any words that I could offer were descriptions, definitions, labels, and characteristics. I had learned that they are true and not true, incomplete, and relative to the hour of the day. I saw two answers to the question. One answer came from my mind, and the other came from my Voice. I could say, "I don't know," and fall head-first into emptiness, or I could say, "I am," and be embraced by its fullness.

There I was, sweeping croissant crumbs onto my napkin and taking the last swig of my now cold coffee. I got up from the table and walked towards the beach with a secret smile on my face. No battle had ensued. Recognizing that I would never recreate my former life allowed me to *stop* pushing away my doubts. They could join me on my path forward, or not, but that's where I was headed no matter what. The tension left my body as I let go of the rope. I floated up into the sky, away from the battleground. I could still see thoughts of doubt lined up like soldiers holding the rope. But without me there, they had nothing to pull against. They dropped the rope, lay down on the grass, looked up at the sky, spotted me, smiled, and waved.

MILESTONES

INNER GUIDANCE

꙳ Doubt lives in the mind and only has power when we also live in our minds.

꙳ Doubt is not the enemy. Doubt does not need to be conquered or eliminated. We can move forward in life with doubt. Indeed, doubt can even point us to wisdom.

꙳ Doubt often creates tension in the body. This tension indicates that there is something else within us that does not agree with the doubt. This "something else" is a deeper wisdom that is not influenced by the mind.

꙳ Slow down here and let your inner wisdom speak in its own time.

DEEPER NAVIGATION

1. Notice when you experience doubt, whether about yourself or something else. How does doubt feel in your body?

2. List the things you usually do when you experience doubt. Think about which things work best, and why.

3. The opposite of doubt is trust. When do you experience self-trust? How does it feel in your body?

13

I AM WHOLE

Danielle in Tulum, Mexico (2018)

I climbed the stairs of the platform nestled in the trees a few feet off a pebble road. Boxes of equipment lined the makeshift stage and needed organizing before the kickoff of the CryptoPsychedelic conference in Tulum, Mexico. What started as a party to celebrate Ted's business partner grew into a weekend full of events, speakers, and DJs in celebration of self-sovereignty in spirit, mind, and economics.

Tulum was the perfect setting for such a gathering as it seemed to be a fast-growing destination for leading-edge entrepreneurs, hippies, and nomads seeking to indulge in transformative experiences in an aquamarine swath of the Gulf of Mexico. The conference was a rare opportunity to bring together wizards of technology and alchemists of the heart. I had never before been surrounded by such a flock of people, each with a beautiful vision for life and each vastly different from the life I knew.

As attendees poured into the space between the trees, I felt that familiar wave of anxiety that comes with large social gatherings. I had no idea how to relate to these people with strong opinions about the world and what they were going to do about it. I was still in the process of untangling myself from corporate life and hadn't yet landed on who I was without it, let alone what came next for the entire species.

The shade of a tree a few feet back offered refuge for observation, and I stepped under it to watch people meet and mingle in the way that always seems effortless from the outside looking in. Despite positioning myself out of the way, a grey-haired man named Isaac introduced himself to me and off I went to perform the theater of small talk. Usually at this point I'm holding a drink in my hand, a prop to fidget with, but that day I had none. I was suddenly aware of how weird it felt to have my hands dangling at my sides.

"Isn't it strange, the way we are taught to socialize?" Isaac said as if he had read my mind. Maybe he had.

I laughed and decided to voice my anxiety, "Why does it feel so strange to stand here and talk without a drink to hold onto? I want to put my hands on my hips or do something with them." I made jazz hands and shook them a bit as my legs kicked a can-can dance. More theater.

Isaac circled his arms in the air, moving them up and down and twirling them around. "We have energy coursing through us, and it wants to go somewhere. So let it go somewhere."

Watching him freely move his body in the middle of a crowd without caring what they thought of his strange display of motion moved something inside of me. Less willing to completely let go of social customs, I wiggled my fingers a little bit and noticed that it felt quite good. I told myself it was okay if people noticed and closed my eyes, allowing my body to move on its own, swaying with the wind.

I opened my eyes and looked at Isaac, "Thank you. I was trapped." I smiled a real smile, one that was inspired from the inside out rather than a conditioned response.

With his hand over his heart, he bowed and said, "Try a hula hoop. It's a much more fun prop than a beer."

What a start to the weekend! Isaac extended a gentle invitation to acknowledge my anxious thoughts without letting them be in charge. I thought I had kicked my mind out of the driver's seat, but it continued to find ways to sneak behind the wheel. It was what I had relied on for decades and I was learning over and over again that while it was an incredible tool, it wasn't leading me where I wanted to go. On the other hand, my intuition's GPS was always perfect. I let it lead the way as my body swayed side to side under the Mexican sun.

When I worked in the corporate world, I had no idea what my intuition was. I had heard the word but had mostly disregarded it as a relic of humanity's ignorant past, like myths about angry Olympian gods to explain the weather that were later replaced by meteorology and Doppler radar. All my choices were based on logic. I was quite good at being rational; hence, I became a lawyer. I could think through situations, see different perspectives, and reason through them all.

As an attorney I thought I had everything figured out, yet I felt utterly confused. It boggled my mind that I was doing what I had been taught to do and yet was still chasing happiness. It always seemed to be one more achievement away. I studied hard, worked hard, and dutifully climbed each rung of the ladder to success. I grabbed every opportunity that came my way, taking internships, executive board positions, and fellowships. When I opened the letter from the law firm inviting me to join their ranks, I thought I had finally reached the top of the ladder.

There I was, a young attorney being asked to work her mind's magic. The offer of a law firm job was a huge badge of honor. I was seen as valuable by an award-winning firm that compensated its employees like kings. I was so proud of myself for earning the opportunity to be the queen of my turf—a 100-square-foot office. *This is it,* I exhaled. This was what I'd been working so hard for. I had proven that I was smart, I was competent, and I was worthy of the space I took up in the world. Surely, happiness would flow into my life now. All I had to do was wait for it to rain down on me. I opened my arms and waited. And waited. And waited. Years went by and I waited. Day after day, week after week, the shine on the badge started to dull.

I spent plenty of time trying to rationalize and reason with myself. Oh, how I tried! I told my discontent all the things it already knew—the salary, the training, the prestige, the set-up for whatever I wanted to do next. It changed nothing. It still wanted my attention.

I was confused, but I didn't know who to ask about it. *Something must have gone wrong as I climbed the ladder,* I thought. I looked around at my peers, my friends, and my colleagues, who had each climbed their own ladder of success and followed the same calculations that I had, and they didn't seem bewildered by their lives. They didn't seem confused or disappointed. I picked apart my life and questioned if I had worked hard enough or if there were more rungs on the ladder left to climb before I earned happiness. No silver bullet revealed itself.

The more I came up empty, the more confused I became, all the while going to my office and billing hundreds of hours with no sense of purpose. I was moving through life on autopilot, with no answers for what had gone wrong, I had no idea how to fix it. The momentum I had created in my career pushed me further up the ladder. I was invited to join committees, given extra pro bono work, and the best partner at the firm was my mentor. Even though the partner-rung on the ladder was years in the future, it was also only ten feet away. I could see the lives of the partners who worked right across the hall from me, and when I thought about someday moving into their offices, my stomach turned. The ladder I had once climbed with hope and vigor had transformed into obligation and resistance.

The world saw me for my resume and validated who I thought I was, so I craved to see myself through other people's eyes. When I looked at myself in the mirror I saw sadness, an empty shell draped in that Ann Taylor suit. The emptiness was where I wasn't. I was living on the edges, on the surface. I was achieving more, amassing more, validating my thinking mind more, but it quite literally wasn't fulfilling me. I couldn't understand my malaise. Why didn't I feel the glory of all that I had achieved? I had created so much success for myself, but I felt like the personification of the word *meh*. I went to my therapist, who told me to talk to my doctor. They both agreed: it was depression. Aha, there was something wrong with me! That was at least an answer. Okay, so I was broken, but my doctor had the fix: antidepressants. The doctor wrote me a script for an SSRI without a second thought.

Holding the script in my hand, relief washed over me. Finally, a solution so that I wouldn't have to feel sad and confused anymore. But I couldn't fill the prescription. I kept avoiding it, which didn't make sense. One day after work I sat down on the couch and rifled through my bag for the script. I had shoved it down to the bottom of the bag, feeling secure that it was there but not wanting to use it. I dug it out, crinkled and a little browned, and smoothed it out in my hands. What to do about this piece of paper?

This tiny note weighed me down. *Why?* Why was I resisting the *solution* to my sadness? Didn't I want to stop feeling sad?

A whisper caressed my ear. "What if how you feel isn't a problem?" the Voice offered gently, delicately to not scare me away like a skittish hummingbird.

"*What?*" I asked.

As if on cue, my Voice came forth. It parted the sea of thoughts that swirled through my mind. It came from somewhere else entirely, not made of the same material as my thoughts at all. Quite plainly, my Voice said, "You're not broken. You're wondering if this prescription will fix you. Your thinking about this is all mixed up. There is nothing to fix. You are not broken," my Voice repeated.

The words permeated my skin, melted through my muscles, trickled into my veins, and flowed through each cell of my body. I was so busy pathologizing myself like a good patient of Western medicine that I hadn't considered that perhaps there was nothing wrong. The cloud of sadness parted, revealing a truth that I had been too distracted by all my anxious thoughts to see: If how I felt wasn't a problem that needed fixing, perhaps *I was not broken.* My stomach unclenched and I exhaled all the stale air I had been holding.

Something that is not broken works exactly as it should. When I felt angry, stressed, or overwhelmed, I was simply experiencing the roller coaster of my thoughts. When I cried, laughed, and screamed into my pillow, I was responding to the power of my perspective. I wasn't broken when I felt depressed. All my attention was being consumed by thoughts I didn't like. I was always responding perfectly to where I placed my attention, on whatever thought it got hooked on, on whatever internal agreements I had unwittingly made. I could feel depressed, angry, and frustrated *and* know I wasn't broken. Knowing that brought a little bit of space, and in that space I could even sneak in a smile.

In the snap of that moment, I stopped believing that how I felt was a problem that needed to be fixed. It didn't mean that all of a sudden I wanted to *keep* feeling depressed, only that I saw it as information rather than as an enemy. My Voice had told me, more through an energetic pulse than through words, that it was not true that how I felt was wrong or bad. If I could see the possibility that it was not wrong or bad, I could open to a whole new outlook in which right and wrong and good and bad weren't relevant and in which the problems created by such judgments didn't exist.

There was nothing wrong with how I had created my life up until that point, and there was nothing wrong with wanting to change it. There was nothing wrong with staying at my job or with taking the prescription if that had been my decision.[1] It was all simply an experience to navigate, and none of it meant I was broken. Looking at the script that still lay in my lap, it had transformed. The heaviness was gone and looked as innocent as a receipt. It could be any scrap of paper. I could take the antidepressants if I wanted, but it wouldn't "fix" anything. There was nothing to fix.

What my Voice had so succinctly communicated through the words "You are not broken," was that my *wholeness* was my birthright. I wasn't empty. I was lost, confused, unsure of myself, but I knew the answers were within me—including the answer to my depression. The answer is always right there next to the question.

Summoning all my skills as an attorney, I realized I had created an internal contract that required me to fulfill various obligations to earn happiness.

I'll be happy when I have a prestigious job.

I'll be happy when I'm successful.

---

[1] Please remember that this is my personal story, my insights and decisions. I am not advocating for any particular choice regarding antidepressants.

I'll be happy when my parents are proud of me.

I'll be happy when I can wear a size two.

I'll be happy when I'm in a committed romantic partnership.

I'll be happy when I'm respected.

I'll be happy when I have no drama in my life.

When I took stock of all these terms, I couldn't believe I had ever signed this agreement. I had given these statements the power to hold me at arm's length from happiness. And the thing was, I *did* achieve these. That's why I was so confused. But when I met each requirement, it upped the ante. I bent over backwards amassing what was required of me, but my outstretched hands remained empty of the reward. Of course, I thought I was broken.

According to my agreement, happiness was an additive experience: I had to achieve and gain and prove myself. By the simple fact that happiness never came, I understood that cobbling my life together from the outside in wasn't working, no matter how hard I pushed.

Happiness is an inside job, and so is everything else. The anger and blame I pinned on my law firm was as much an illusion as the happiness it was supposed to offer. They were born of different agreements I had made with myself about how I was "supposed" to show up at work and how work was "supposed" to show up for me. These agreements covered everything, even how I was "supposed" to show up at social gatherings—standing still with a drink in my hand. All these contracts that required the world to be a certain way for me to be okay were not only untrue, but also splintered me from my wholeness.

I was now in the position to renegotiate my happiness, so what did I want to change? I struck all the terms that required me to do, prove, or achieve anything. I peeled off the layers of my mental noise, the "musts" and "shoulds" that directed how I created my life.

"You are not broken" was the four-word key to my new contract. Because I was not broken, I was okay exactly as I was. Happiness was not an additive experience but a subtractive one. Striking through all the terms I had imposed on myself left me with nothing to do, change, or fix. I was *allowed* to be happy right *now*.

I did *not* need to have a prestigious job to be deserving.

I did *not* need to achieve more.

I did *not* need to make my parents proud.

I did *not* need to do what was expected of me.

I did *not* need to label my choices as good or bad.

My new contract had no terms. It simply said, "I can be happy now." My hands trembled as the power of this new agreement settled into my body. My chest expanded as if I had taken my first full breath since I was a kid. *This* is who I am! Under the terms of this new agreement, I was free to make choices in life from a different perspective that didn't require proving anything. I had given myself permission to feel happy *now*, which put me in a much better position to decide what to do next. Decisions made from fear and obligation were never my best. Simply knowing that this was my new orientation for life brought me more happiness than I had felt in a long time.

I stared in the mirror over the bathroom sink at the empty shell inside my suit without grimacing or looking away. My hollowness transformed from scary to sacred. In that space lived my desire to know what it meant to live a life that I truly wanted. But I had no idea what that was. It was a question I had never even considered. No one had left a trail of crumbs for me to follow. I had no idea what to do with myself after I announced my resignation from the law firm. I had no plan.

What became so obvious as I twirled in the jungle of Tulum was that I did know exactly what to do: keep looking at myself in the mirror and honoring the space behind my eyes as sacred.

It's in moments like these that I lean on the tremendous power of the simple words, "I am not broken." These words send bolts of energy sizzling up my spine, always reorienting me towards my true nature. The girl dancing in the trees. This girl lets her body's intuition lead the way. She knows there are no terms for life, for work, or for mingling at a party. There is nothing to figure out, change, or prove. In any situation, the only thing we need to ask is, "What do I want to do from here?" In this simple question is the full acceptance of where we are now—no judgment good or bad—and the freedom to choose what comes next.

MILESTONES

INNER GUIDANCE

- Our inner wisdom tells us we are perfect as we are. We are not broken.
- Because we are not broken, there is nothing to fix or change.
- When we turn our focus from our self-generated mental noise about who we "need" to be and tune into our inner wisdom, we come to understand our wholeness.
- We are working perfectly, even when we are in the throes of stress and overwhelm. This is what we are meant to feel when we are experiencing our revved-up thoughts.
- Life cannot cause us to "break." It can only cause us to experience feelings (like fear, sadness, and anger) in response to our thoughts.
- Feelings are meant to be felt. We are not broken when we feel our feelings, especially the difficult ones.

DEEPER NAVIGATION

1. When do you find it easiest to listen to your inner voice? When do you find yourself silencing your inner voice?
2. What does wholeness mean to you? Take some time to reflect on moments in your life when you felt whole. These are times when you felt at ease with yourself and didn't try to fix or achieve anything. What circumstances invite you to settle into this sense of ease? What were you doing? What was your headspace and heart space?
3. Close your eyes and picture the face of someone who loves, appreciates, and approves of you. Notice how they look at you, the way their eyes gaze at you and how their mouth settles into a relaxed smile. Step into the body of this person and look behind their eyes and feel how they feel. Embody the love and appreciation they feel for you. There's nothing to do here, simply soak up this feeling for a minute or two.

Remember this feeling of wholeness—satisfaction without need or expectation—is always available to you.

4. Imagine you were more at ease with yourself than you are now. How would you sit? How would you speak? What would your voice sound like? What kinds of thoughts would you have?

5. Refer to the internal agreements you wrote down in Chapter 5. Knowing what you know now, are there any agreements that you want to change? Even 1%? One percent can make a huge difference, so do not overlook what is now possible, even if it seems small.

14

I AM SAFE

Danielle at Mount Cook National Park, New Zealand (2018)

When Ted and I stepped off the plane in Christchurch, a city in New Zealand's South Island, the first thing I noticed was how good it felt to breathe. The air was fresh and crisp, and I gulped it down. *This* is what breathing was supposed to feel like. It was a far cry from the headache-inducing smog in Hanoi. It was life-giving. New Zealand stole my heart when it filled my lungs.

We spent our first night on a ten-acre, family-run vineyard in a tiny one-street town called Rangiora on the edge of Christchurch. The land was beautiful, rolling hills dotted with cows, sheep, and grapes. We spent

New Year's Eve day exploring the region's vineyards, tasting Pinot Noirs and Rieslings. We constantly crisscrossed the road in our rented SUV as we remembered after each stop to pull out to the left.

New Year's Eve, overhyped as it is, usually underdelivers. Because I was used to the hoopla of New Year's Eve in the States, I made reservations ahead of time at a local restaurant called The Plough and dolled myself up in my sparkliest shirt for the festivities. Boy, did I look like an idiot. We arrived at the town pub that was really an old converted barn, not in a modern-yet-kitschy way, but more like a patched-up job from 1861. For the residents of this agricultural town, dominated by hunting, fishing, and sheep shearing, New Year's Eve apparel consisted of fishing hats and AC/DC t-shirts sporting sloshed pints of beer. Even though the crowd may have looked like a Memphis biker bar, there was no rough and tumble here. A band played for the occasion, mostly cover songs from a range of American classics like CCR, Elvis, and Sublime. The frontman was in his fifties with a bald head and a silver beard down to his collarbone. He had a rumbling voice and killed it on the tambourine.

Then off on the road we went. Ted and I cruised the entire island, exploring its natural majesty: hiking glaciers and mountains, swimming at beaches and lakes, and kayaking fjords and glowworm-filled caves. We'd stop every 500 meters to take a photo of sheep or a snow-capped mountain, and sometimes simply to breathe the air and skip a few rocks.

We had to scoop our jaws off the floor when we arrived at Lake Tekapo, a body of glacial water surrounded by rolling hills of evergreen trees. Directly behind the lake sits snowy Mount Cook, whose peak kisses the clouds. The lake is a bluish turquoise depending on the sunlight, never failing to contrast beautifully against the reddish-orange hills. My eyes hungrily darted back and forth, up and down, eager to take it all in. A field of lavender grew by the lake, and I plopped down to soak it up, absorbing the beauty of this place into my skin. The landscape left me dazzled and soothed at the same time. It was awesome in the cosmic sense of the word. Man could not make this.

I wished I could have stretched my arms around its vastness, but its awesomeness came exactly from the fact that I couldn't. The expansive view reflected my own expansion since relaxing my tight grip on life. It was a perfect setting to reflect on what I wanted for the New Year. Here in the rugged wilderness of lakes and sheep, there were no expectations to live up to. Only my own, and my own were quickly shifting like the tectonic plates far beneath me. I felt the cocoon I had wrapped around myself in D.C. starting to open. My wings began to flutter as I thought about what it looked like to create life on *my* terms.

I wasn't as bewildered by the question as when I had been staring at my reflection in the bathroom sink. I was beginning to feel like maybe I knew what a few of my terms were. Because there was nothing I needed to fix, change, or do, I was safe to play with life however I wanted.

Safety had always been my north star. I followed wherever it took me. As a twenty-one-year-old college graduate, the vast unknown had stretched out in front of me, and I trembled at its grandness. I had no idea how I was supposed to navigate the landscape safely and arrive at the oasis of success. Gathering my courage and my wits, I plowed forward, never mind that I didn't know where I was headed.

It was 2009, smack in the middle of the economic and housing collapse. The job market for recent grads had been greatly impacted. Some of my friends were unemployed for a year or more, while others had been hired and fired within a few short months. I had moved to a new city and had no community or contacts, except for a few friends that I hadn't spoken to since elementary school. Through one of those friends, I got a job at her mortgage company. I really didn't know what I wanted to do and getting experience at a "real job" felt like the most immediate goal. I felt safe.

The feeling didn't last long. I knew this wasn't my career path. I felt pressured to figure out what that was and how to navigate getting there in a depressed economy. After a few months I once again felt lost, untethered, without purpose or direction. I was wasting time, and wasting time felt lazy. Lazy wasn't safe.

With parents who are themselves attorneys, I was inclined to attend law school. Choosing law school accomplished two things: it pulled me out of the economy by putting me back in school, a lifeline in itself, and it gave me the opportunity to kick the can of deciding what I wanted to do with my life. Law school famously gives you a degree without a stated purpose by sharpening skills that can be used in a variety of career paths. Attending law school offered me the critical ability to say, "I'm in law school," which implied future success. I felt safe.

After law school, I was drawn to the law firm job like a moth to a flame. How much safer could I be than embraced by the ivory tower of the industry? In their ranks, I suddenly became incredibly financially stable for a twenty-something-year-old with no dependents, no car, and no mortgage. I felt safe telling anyone I met what I did and where I worked. No one could say that I wasn't smart, I wasn't driven, or that I hadn't become successful. I was safe from any looks of disappointment that I wasn't living up to my potential.

And that's when the Voice started to speak to me, whispering in my ear for years before finally calling loudly to me during the biggest trial of my career. The trial had worked me harder than I had ever worked before. I slept in three or four-hour blocks for weeks at a time. There was no time for self-care, exercise, cooking healthy food, or tending to anything else in my life. It was no surprise that I caught a cold, with a runny nose, foggy brain, and hacking cough that rumbled the courtroom. I couldn't afford to rest and heal. I had to keep going. The wrath of the partners who sat beside me every day was much too intimidating.

Looking back at the experience, I saw that I had to run myself down to the point where I couldn't press on any longer, giving me no choice but to surrender and listen to the Voice. When it said, "Danielle, you aren't here," it made no sense, because of course I was there. I saw my feet squeezed into my black pumps, my chest rising and falling inside my shirt, the creases and folds in my palms. Here I was, wasn't I?

But I couldn't shoo the Voice away, and when I finally listened, I understood. The words weren't pointing to my physical location. They were pointing to that invisible space in my heart where all I desired lived and thrived . . . and I wasn't there to experience it. I had navigated the path as an attorney out of a need to feel safe, but in doing so it had taken me out of my heart, sapped my energy, and drained my inspiration. *That's* why I felt depressed. I wasn't where I wanted to be. Seeking safety had brought me to a place that assuaged fear but offered no inspiration. Yes, I could afford fancy clothes, and yes, my parents were proud. And yes, I was miserable and confused. The overwhelming lack of satisfaction in my life forced me to look in the mirror at who I had become.

The safety I cultivated through tireless work and careful choices was only an illusion, a fortress built against the enemy of my own projection. I was living up to what I thought others expected of me as a dutiful daughter, professional, and woman. I would never feel safe from wondering if I was living up to their expectations. When I quit my job, I wriggled free of this false safety.

Like most of us, I was acculturated to believe I could control life by creating something stable and sturdy out of degrees and glossy hair. It's why politicians, if they can't exert control over some aspect of society's problems, demand more power. Quite frankly, this is nonsense. The COVID-19 pandemic that began in 2020 showed us that our external safety is only an illusion, a house made of straw, no match for what life may have in store. Humanity endured this huge wake-up call as jobs were eliminated, economies decimated, lives shattered, and families heartbroken. All the external aspects of safety were knocked down in one fell swoop.

Sitting in the great expansiveness of Lake Tekapo, I saw natural safety. I was fully safe to be me whether I summited Mount Cook or sat at its feet, fingers full of dirt. I would be me, connected and whole, regardless of where I stood in the world. I was safe no matter what I chose to do with my life. Whether or not I wore an Ann Taylor suit. I was no longer fooled into believing I was safest only when standing on the mountain peak.

If I was *safe* to be me, no matter what, then following whatever my terms for life were—even if they made everyone around me uncomfortable— posed no *risk*. The tenuous feeling of vulnerability that came from sticking my neck out and forging my own path was real only if I believed safety came from following the standard path. The truth was that staying on that path felt riskier than leaving it behind. Sitting in that lavender field, I unwound myself from others' expectations, untangled them from my heart and liver and mind, and exhaled them out of my body.

If I could do whatever I wanted, be whoever I wanted, what did that look like? A new "term" for my life burst forth from my heart and lodged itself in the sky as my new north star: to live a life that *inspired* me. The pull of inspiration would navigate my path forward. It didn't really matter what inspired me or where it took me because the destination wasn't the point. There was nothing to achieve by arriving anywhere. The purpose in each moment was no more complex than to follow inspiration. Period. Doing this would take me wherever I was supposed to be. That felt like the safest life of all.

MILESTONES

INNER GUIDANCE

> ❧ We tend to build our sense of safety through the external world, but such safety is only an illusion. Life can bring circumstances to our doorstep that demolish all the external aspects of safety we rely on.

> ❧ True safety comes from within. It is always within us, and it is up to us to connect to it. When we relax into our wholeness, we connect with our safety.

> ❧ When we understand that we are always safe, we are empowered to take more risks in life. What may have once felt scary or impossible may no longer feel out of reach.

DEEPER NAVIGATION

1. We tend to have an adult version of a child's safety blanket, something or someone whose presence makes us feel safe. Reflect on what your adult safety blankets are. It could be a number on your bank statement or the color of your hair.

2. What are your safety blankets protecting you from? After you write down your answers, go another layer deeper. *Why* do you need protection from these things? Go another layer deeper and ask yourself *Why* again.

3. Think of someone who you consider to be confident. How do they walk, sit, stand, smile, and breathe? How do they talk and what do they say? What words do they use? How do they move? Imagine stepping into this person and seeing through their eyes, using their words, sitting how they sit, feeling how they feel. What are you willing to do or say from here?

4. What would you do if you knew you couldn't fail? Think big. There is no inspiration in thinking small.

15

I AM RESILIENT

Danielle and Ted in the Hang E Cave, Phong Nha, Vietnam (2017)

"It was muddier a few days ago," our guide said as we pursued an exit strategy from the dense, wet jungle. I thought that was entirely impossible. My feet were drenched in mud despite my boots being specifically designed for this terrain. Brown water splashed the entire length of my pants; I was soaked from intermittent rainfall even though I was dressed like a Northface commercial. Good thing it wasn't summer because I was already starting to sweat in my rain gear. I really wasn't sure why I was bothering to wear it. *Oh right*, I remembered, protection from the poisonous plants growing at the trail's edge.

Each step forward was deliberate. I gingerly climbed over broken tree trunks and held onto branches for support as my confidence in my ability to keep vertical waned. I ice-skated through the slippery jungle, keeping my feet wide and my arms out for balance. The mud slurped my feet deeper as I slogged forward.

I pulled something in my leg when I jerked it away from a slippery rock and prayed it wasn't serious as I marched onward. Rain had started to fall again, offering a soothing soundtrack in contrast with my agonizing thoughts. My back hurt from leaning forward with my pack to fit through the semi-cleared sloshy path. Ted told the guide he was going to take a few steps off the trail to pee and the guide whipped his head around and rebuked, "Absolutely not." In addition to the poisonous plants, venomous snakes, and jaguars in the jungle, there were thousands of unexploded ordinances, gruesome relics of the Vietnam War lying in wait only a few feet off the trail that hadn't yet been "cleared." No problem, he could wait to pee.

I had signed up for this day-long adventure, an act of courageous tourism to hike the recently opened Ho Chi Minh trails in Phong Nha, Vietnam, previously trekked by the Viet Cong. I was hungry. My body had burned through its morning supply of fuel. My legs resisted my brain's order to lift off the ground and carry my sack of bones over gnarled roots and rocks. My mind was the tired commander of an exhausted body. I was battling a fear I pretended not to have of slipping and tumbling off a cliff.

The Dark Cave revealed itself slowly as the thick leaves and branches gave way to a clearing. Relieved for a break from the rain, I put on my headlamp to light my way. We splashed through a freezing thigh-high river at the mouth of the cave and stepped up onto a sandy floor surrounded by huge, craggy limestones stretching three or four meters high. The only way in was up, climbing over the sharp rocks into the dead of darkness. The rocks weren't only sharp, they were slippery from the drips falling from the calcium deposits on the cave's ceiling. Great. I climbed over the rocks in pitch black except for the pinhole of dim light offered by my headlamp.

I swallowed down a minor anxiety attack. Why was I doing this? I considered myself athletic. I had a personal record of deadlifting 265 pounds. I'd mastered pull-ups, my endurance was great, and I could face the impossible and crush it. But I really didn't want to do this. I was scared.

I imagined the Viet Cong using this cave as a welcome refuge and steeled my nerves.

After exiting the Dark Cave, we hiked deeper into the jungle, sloshing through murky rivers while watching for leeches, stomping through mud made thicker from the rain, and stepping gingerly to avoid getting my feet caught in roots and vines hidden under the sludge. I had brought along my fancy Nikon camera under the assumption I'd be taking amazing photos of this historic trail, but it quickly became dead weight in my pack. Every neuron in my brain and every atom of my body was focused on staying upright and moving.

The rain let up as we arrived at a narrow river, which we followed to the mouth of the Hang E Cave. This was a water cave, the guide told us, meaning we'd be swimming through it. He pointed down at his boots and tugged off his jacket, signaling to take off any layers I didn't want to get wet. *Wet?* What wasn't already soaking? I let out a big sigh. Off with the layers of jackets, pants, boots, and socks, and on with the headlamp. I slid down the riverbank and waded into the crystal-clear turquoise water. With my headlamp on, I frog-legged into the dark hollow as the water turned cold and then freezing with no light to warm it. A current pulled me deeper into the cave. Was the water flowing inward? It was dark, confusing, and magical. Peaceful and silent, I couldn't tell if my eyes were open or closed.

Swimming out of the cave, I came face to face with the horror of putting on my wet socks and muddy boots—damp, slimy, and caked with sludge. Why was I carrying this stupid brick of a camera around when I should have brought a fresh pair of socks? Hands shaking from the cold, putting on my socks proved quite a challenge. I focused on each sock like a bull at a matador, charging my foot at the listless cloth I held open with my hands. After a quick bite of food, we headed back into the jungle.

The sky hovered menacingly over the jungle valley. Whatever sun wasn't covered by clouds barely found its way down here. Should I turn my headlamp on again? I was starting to limp from whatever muscle I had pulled and avoided putting weight on my right leg. I pushed forward, feeling drier and more hopeful after some time passed beneath the sun, when the clouds opened up again and pellets of rain began to fall. The sky turned a deep grey, and a chill ran through me as the sun started to set. *I can do it*, I kept thinking. *I must keep going. I'm not staying in the jungle.*

After another hour and a half of dreary marching, a clearing emerged and I recognized there were only about three hundred meters left. I made it out alive! Not one hundred percent, but my muscle would heal and a hot shower and a big meal awaited me. I was exhausted but proud of finishing this trek and experiencing a place that is hidden from most of the world.

I had volunteered for this "hike in the jungle," and paid money to trek the twelve kilometers of the Ho Chi Minh trail. Only in the last few years had these incredible cave complexes been opened to tourism. Where I had spent only a day, Vietnamese soldiers lived every day and night, summer and winter, until the war ended. No hot shower had awaited them. It's strange to do for "fun" what these soldiers had done to survive.

Every time my leg hurt and I wanted to quit, well, what choice did I have? There was no other way out of the jungle, only forward. I kept thinking of the mud that covered the boots of those who had walked the trail before me and the physical, mental, and emotional stress the men had endured without respite when injuries or illnesses befell them. Here I was, roasting by the fire in dry clothes, sipping ginger tea, and telling the tale to another tourist who had plunked down next to me with a hot cocoa and asked about my day. I couldn't say it had been fun, but it had been worth it.

The tourist I shared my harrowing tale with said, "And you're more resilient for it!" I received her kindness with a smile, but I had learned that wasn't the way it worked. We are taught that we gain resiliency through adversity, that it must be earned and achieved along the way.

As our experience of life is generated from the inside out, it is impossible for an external experience to build us up or tear us down. When we are stressed, depressed, and confused, we search for clarity, confidence, and calm. We look for something to help us deal with whatever is going on— death, divorce, an empty bank account, or a treacherous hike. The nature of the stress is not actually the number in the bank account or the mud on our boots, but our *thinking* about it. Typically, those thoughts reveal an insecurity with our ability to cope. My stress on the trail that day wasn't really about my cold wet socks or my strained muscle; it was in response to my insecurity about how I would deal with them. The real question I was asking was: *Will I survive?*

What is adversity, really, other than our insecurity about our ability to thrive in a situation? The heart of the matter is always pointing us back to ourselves. As much as it might seem like our stress and overwhelm is caused by what's happening outside of us, this is an illusion. The unpleasant emotions we feel during life's challenges are always related to our *confidence* in our ability to thrive.

Deep in the Vietnamese jungle full of unexploded bombs and feline predators, I came face-to-face with my resilience. Navigating this challenge had me doubting my ability to cope. What I most desired in the world that day was not a fresh pair of socks or a hot dog, but an unshakable trust that I would be okay. Not having dry clothes or an instant fix for my pulled muscle left me two options: freak out or buck up. To me, "buck up" doesn't really mean to grit my teeth and face into the wind, but to lean into trusting that I am capable of more than I realize. *I can do this.*

It's not that we receive more resiliency through life's challenges, but that we tap into what's already there. Nestled inside ourselves is creativity, determination, persistence, curiosity, and hope. These are a few of the qualities of our innate resiliency, our capacity to thrive. In adverse situations, we intuitively tap into this birthright as it is the natural intelligence woven into the fabric of our being.

This is how we learned to walk as babies, determined to explore, with unwavering tenacity to try again when we fell down. As we grow up, we ask more from life. The desire to walk turns into a desire to run and jump, and eventually we ask to fly. Life brings us new, bigger opportunities to explore our innate capabilities. Each time we navigate adversity, we trust that we can handle what is asked of us, even if the next time life will ask more of us. It is not our resiliency that we are building, but our *confidence* in ourselves. There is no gap in our innate abilities, only in our self-trust as we navigate each of life's challenges. Each moment of insecurity is an opportunity to forge a deeper relationship to self-trust.

MILESTONES

INNER GUIDANCE

❧ We are capable of more than we realize.

❧ Resiliency is not something that we earn. Resiliency is our birthright, a part of our natural intelligence. We are built to thrive.

❧ When we navigate life's challenges, we tap into this resilience. Each time we move through a challenge, we prove to ourselves how resilient we are.

❧ When we feel stressed about a challenge we are facing, we are experiencing thoughts of insecurity about our ability to cope. This insecurity is our desire for more self-trust. We want an unshakable confidence in our ability to thrive.

DEEPER NAVIGATION

1. Take some time to reflect on some of the challenges you've faced from childhood to the present day. Notice that no matter how insecure or doubtful you felt, your innate ability to thrive showed up, as you are here now.

2. Be forensic about how your ability to thrive shows up for you. What does it look like? Courage, hope, surrender, creativity? The more you see that these innate faculties are always "on," the more you will relax into life.

16

I AM GRACE

Danielle in Esalen, Big Sur, California (2018)

A few months into backpacking, I decided I was "officially" a spiritual person. The inward journey investigating who I was took me to incredible places where massive amounts of wisdom waited for me. The more I learned about myself, the more I learned about the world, and vice versa. This was a nourishment I had not previously experienced along the linear path of traditional education. It was like arriving at an oasis of peaches, coconuts, and miso soup after a lifetime of floating on a leaky raft sustained by soy shakes and protein bars.

I happily pruned my former identity as a hard worker, lawyer, Jew, and American, and tended to my new identity as spiritual. Soon, new questions arose. What did spiritual people do? How do they practice spirituality? Was there a way to be officially spiritual? How does one mark themselves to be seen by others as spiritual? Should I buy white flowy clothes and mala beads? Should I get a tattoo of the moon or a chakra or something in Sanskrit? Should I start meditating every day and stop drinking alcohol? At the very least, should I update my LinkedIn profile photo so it would no longer show me in an Ann Taylor suit?

I expected to find a path to follow, a linear succession of steps, a checklist of achievements to point to, so I could measure my progress as a spiritual person. Religions are full of checklists. Going to church on Sunday is a simple act that doesn't require much to prove you're Christian. Simply *going* to church says, "You belong here. You are one of us." Even easier is getting a Christmas tree! If you do nothing all year except place this triangular pine tree in your living room in December, voila! You're part of the club. I never had a Christmas tree despite really wanting one as a kid because that's simply not something most Jews do. It was a bright line indicator of where I belonged.

What did spiritual people do? I wondered how I could signal to the world that I was part of this club. There are some mainstream answers to this question. Some of the most popular ones I ran into were meditation, yoga, breath work, collecting crystals, holding ceremonies around moon cycles, and medicinal plant use (entheogens—psychoactive substances like cannabis, psilocybin, and peyote). I feasted at the all-you-can-eat buffet of spiritual modalities, stacking my plate with a little bit of this and a helping of that. I skipped the things I didn't know how to eat (astrology and enneagram) and watched how other people chewed on what was on their plates, like spiritual philosophy from Alan Watts and Ken Wilber.

As I met more and more people with a spiritual practice (that they all swore by), I learned more and more modalities to try.

"First thing in the morning I sit quietly in my garden for twenty minutes and listen to binaural beats. Then I move through my yoga practice, followed by nourishing my body with a green smoothie with ashwagandha and lemons from my garden. Then I check my email!"

"Every morning I hike down to a waterfall and pray to the goddess Guan Yin."

"Before I get out of bed, with my eyes still closed, I visualize everyone in my family and send them love.

"I keep a small journal by my bed and before I go to sleep at night, I write down five things from the day that I am grateful for."

I put pressure on myself to build a practice that showed evidence of my new spiritual identity. I could confidently say, "See? I do this and that, so I am spiritual." Without realizing it, I had sneakily inserted dogma into my new identity: "I must have a way of showing I am spiritual." This wasn't true. My mind was back at its old tricks in a new context, trying to prove who I was from the outside in.

What was true was that I was on an unmarked path. No one had forced me to start this journey, and no one could tell me whether I was doing it right or wrong. The unwinding of my labels and stories without expectations or goals was my spirituality. My spiritual "practice" was whatever allowed me to unwind, whether that was tarot cards or swimming laps or drinking a cup of coffee.

I had a giggle. These stories I kept bumping up against were a reminder of my humanity. Part of being human is having a mind, and our minds are on a constant quest to tell us the story of our lives. There's no need to rid ourselves of stories, and we'd be about as successful at it as peeling off our skin. As tender gardeners of our minds, it would be constant backbreaking work to prune them of stories. There is a spiritual concept of *transcendence*—the notion that the path to true spiritual enlightenment is up and out of ourselves, meaning pursuit of detachment from all stories. To transcend is to ascend out of messy earthiness and our physicality—the forms that keep us tied to suffering—so we can rocket up and away into the cosmos, where none of this dirty human business exists. Where, they say, we can truly be free.

But in my bones I know that spirituality is an embodied practice, meaning that it embraces being part of this world. There is no need to leave it behind to experience full connection to the divine. Why have a garden if nothing is allowed to grow? The experience of spirituality is in the cracks and crevices of everyday life—holding the hand of your beloved as you sit at the movie theater, washing dishes and feeling the warm suds slipping over your fingers, singing at the top of your lungs with your hair whipping in the wind as you cruise down the highway, sitting with your dying grandfather and watching him hold on and let go over and over again. The reality is we are born into bodies with minds, so a major component of human spirituality includes all the messiness of physical and mental life.

However, because we are the tender gardeners of our lives, we get to decide what stories belong on our grounds and which are weeds to be plucked. This is why I call myself spiritual. There are no rules about how your garden needs to look. There is nothing you must do or mantra you must say or creed you must believe. There is no intermediary, no rabbi or shaman or imam or priest who can validate or chastise you. It is direct connection to the sacred. It's your inner wisdom, your higher self, God, universal consciousness, the divine, intuition, energy. No one can tell you how to get there or what it is you are getting to. It's your experience. It's your garden.

I took a quick trip to Austin, Texas, to attend a Christmas party full of folks I had met along my journey. A lovely young man came up to me whom I had met once before at Esalen, a conscious-hippie retreat center in Big Sur, California, and I had very much enjoyed getting to know him. Despite his youth, he exuded a graceful confidence and was unafraid of being quiet and listening to conversation rather than elbowing his way in. I often noticed him not saying anything but watching, clearly present with all that unfolded. We caught up with where our travels had taken us and where we were going next, and it quickly evolved to sharing our journeys with spirituality—what we were currently sitting with, what we were exploring, what wisdom was coming through for us.

He exuded a zest for life. His eyes lit up as he shared with me that he was finding so much inspiration. I nodded along excitedly, wanting to share in his child-like wonder of what life offered. As I asked him questions about his spiritual journey, he told me that he credited it to a big change he made in his life based on his mentor's recommendation.

"What was his recommendation?" I asked, hungrily wanting in on the secret.

"I stopped eating meat," he replied matter-of-factly.

I was never good at hiding my emotions and my eyebrows scrunched together in confusion. I had not been expecting something so mundane. Vegetarianism and all kinds of different diets are popular, so it wasn't a shocking spiritual practice, but it was shocking coming from *him*. This wise, quiet man who so obviously spent most of his time inside his mind and heart was telling me he had gained access to enlightened awareness by no longer eating hamburgers.

At this point in my journey, I had a very devotional practice of the Japanese energy healing modality called Reiki. I learned all about the framework of the chakra system. *Chakras* are the spinning energy centers of the body (chakra means "wheel" in Sanskrit). The seven major chakras move upwards from the base of the spine to the top of our heads.

The chakra system teaches that certain foods are associated with each energy center. Meat is associated with our root chakra, the lowest of the seven chakras. The base chakra is called the *root* because it's tied to grounding and stability. It is our connection to the Earth, the cradle of life. It brings us a sense of safety in the world, and our right to take up space here. As we rise through our higher chakras, towards more ethereal things like ideas, vision, and imagination in our third-eye and crown chakras, the foods associated with them become lighter. In fact, according to author and somatic therapist Anodea Judith[2], the foods associated with the third-eye chakra are entheogens that provide access to an expanded perspective. There is no food associated with the crown chakra. At that chakra, one is fasting or detoxing toxins and chemicals out of the system.

My knowledge led me to infer that perhaps his mentor's recommendation had come from the notion that to ascend into his higher chakras, he needed to let go of a food that kept him grounded. I imagined a big juicy steak tied to the end of a balloon, weighing it down so it couldn't float away.

The Christmas party was held at one of Austin's most famous BBQ spots and the menu was essentially brisket, ribs, turkey, and a few sides. Ted and I shared a joke that in Texas even the vegetables are not vegetarian. I chowed down on my BBQ brisket, wiping sauce from my cheeks, while this young man munched on some green beans and extolled the value of not eating meat. I swallowed my surprise and urged him to

---

2   *Wheels of Life: A User's Guide to the Chakra System* by Anodea Judith (Llewellyn Publications, 1987).

continue sharing his experience of vegetarianism. What he told me next was astonishing. He told me that people *could not* access enlightenment if they ate meat.

You know how sometimes in cartoons a character like Bugs Bunny will be running through the forest with Elmer Fudd on his tail? Bugs will suddenly skid to a stop and the grass underneath him will ruffle up underneath his feet. That's how I felt. The rhythm and flow of our conversation came to a sudden halt. I was completely thrown off. It was one thing for this young man to share his journey with me and for me to be surprised by his choices, but entirely different for him to tell me he had embraced a certain dogma about spirituality: *you must not eat meat to become enlightened.* The only absolute that I knew to be true was that there were no rules. Even in that I saw the irony.

I didn't know what to say, so I cheekily waved my fork at him, implying that here I was fully carnivorous and unwilling to believe that I could not access my own enlightenment. If I were to believe his dietary restriction, it would invalidate my own spiritual experiences. Not to mention those of everyone else who eats meat. I wanted to poke at him a little bit to get under the hood. What I understood was that he was having such a profound, rich, and beautiful experience, which he attributed to abstaining from meat, that he was convinced that accessing this inspired state was not available any other way. His story was really a blind devotional tribute to the access vegetarianism gave him to his true self. He was so deep in the delicious throes of living that he could not step outside it to witness the projection of his perspective as a static objective truth that applied to everyone.

At the time I thought how superior I was to my poor friend who was caught in a web of his own making. I was free of webs because I knew there was no dogma in spirituality, and this knowledge kept me free and clear of getting stuck. But what I've since come to understand was that my judgment of this man was my story, a cross to bear of my own making. My curiosity about my friend's experience was an agenda for judgment and my compassion for his journey was a cloak for pity. I felt proud that I had not made such a detour into dogma.

There was a story rattling around in my brain that I hadn't the space to see. Much later I found it, not at all on purpose. I was gardening a rosebush when I spotted a vine. I followed this vine across the garden, entangling itself with every tree and flower. It fed and fed off everything that grew, choking what didn't. The vine was a belief that there is a better and a worse way to move through the journey of life: *efficiently*. I believed efficiency was good and detours were bad. I had escaped going off course by avoiding the dogmatic pitfall of not eating meat or grandstanding that everyone must abstain from meat. But the pride I felt in avoiding that pitfall showed me the value I had placed on efficiency.

I loved transforming as fast as I could; any detour or slow down felt like failure, a waste of time. Efficiency was my vegetarianism. I had projected a story onto my friend in the same way that he had projected his onto me. The only difference was that I wasn't even aware I held this belief. I couldn't fathom that perhaps his dogmatic diet was not a detour at all. Perhaps there was something in this experience that offered my friend a quantum leap forward on his path that would have taken him much longer or more suffering if he had not rejected meat on behalf of the world. Or even more outrageous, perhaps it was okay for him to simply take a detour.

In the wise words of Ram Dass, my friend and mentor, "When you have the compassion that comes from understanding how it is, you don't lay a trip on anybody else as to how they ought to be." When I realized my own story and saw it for what it was, I felt true grace both for my friend and for myself. Simply, neither of us was ready to catch ourselves in our dogma. At least he knew what his dogma was, whereas I hadn't recognized mine until years later.

We simply can't see the stories that define our perspectives . . . until we can. And that's okay. Let it be a game of "I Spy," because *why not?* The process is never done, so don't turn it into a chore with a goal to prune all the weeds. See what you notice about who you are and what makes up your perspective. Just *noticing* it can be enough.

I've not pruned out efficiency. I've simply reflected on it and noticed how it appears sometimes as a weed and sometimes as a beautiful oak tree. I love efficiency and I leverage it in my work. I've also come to notice when my drive to be efficient is wearing me out and I need a break. In the universe's perfectly playful fashion, slowing down often can be the most efficient thing to do as the slowing down offers clarity more quickly than blindly forging ahead. Since I don't know what the future holds, my judgment of whether something is moving along efficiently is an illusion anyway. My relationship to efficiency has become dynamic and alive, and it's allowed me to let go of imposing it on others.

When we notice our stories, we can decide what to do about them. Play with them, experiment with them, notice how they show up in life, embrace them, or do away with them if that seems right. If what we want to do about it changes, great. We can always change our minds.

MILESTONES

INNER GUIDANCE

- We create the rules, or dogma, to which we subscribe. They are always created from within us.
- It's human nature to create dogma and project it onto the world around us.
- The rules we create can be hard to spot. We may see them right away or take a lifetime to notice.
- Awareness of our rules gives us the conscious ability to do something about them.
- We don't need to change the rules we notice. We don't need to keep them or get rid of them. We can play with how we use them in our lives.

DEEPER NAVIGATION

1. As you go about your day, notice when something strikes you as right or wrong. These moments are clues about the rules you live by. Be forensic here, paying attention to the details. You may start to see patterns about how you create the rules for your life.

2. Many of our rules for life are inherited and we live by them without a second thought. When you notice a rule, write it down and reflect on *why* you live by this rule. Sometimes the why arrives easily, and sometimes it's just a vague feeling. If you don't know why and there's no strong feeling, notice this too. What might it indicate?

3. As you notice more about how you create the rules for your life, you'll notice that other people do this as well. Notice how everyone behaves according to their own rules. How does your awareness of this impact your relationships?

~~ **PART IV** ~~

TRANSFORMATION

Personal transformation can and does have global effects.
As we go, so goes the world, for the world is us. The revolution
that will save the world is ultimately a personal one.

—MARIANNE WILLIAMSON

17

I AM NOW

Danielle in Porto, Portugal (2018)

We arrived in Porto, a coastal city in the north of Portugal, on a whim. Unlike the beginning of our travels when I researched everything about a location, the urge to know what I was getting into had disappeared. The coast of Portugal boasts a sunny temperate climate that kisses your cheeks late into fall, which was good enough for us. Off we went.

A year of travel feels like it spans an entire Chinese dynasty. There's so much newness, so much to take in, so much to get used to. There's hardly time to get into a routine, let alone get bored. By the time we headed for Porto, we were scrambling to screenshot some simple Portuguese phrases on our phones before turning them on airplane mode. We had done no research about the city and had no understanding of the history or the geopolitical circumstances we might find ourselves in. "Pack and go" had become our modus operandi.

Narrow cobblestone streets cradled old-world nostalgia. Maybe a city could build a six-lane highway made of cobblestone and still feel quaint, but there is probably a reason no such highway exists. The presence of cobblestones signals a pace of life that cannot quicken beyond what the stones allow.

The buildings are a mismatch of rococo churches and row houses. Stretching down the street are lines of four-story buildings, each with distinct tilework and staggered balconies. The row house façades are dressed in thousands of individual square tiles painted blue, purple, and white with yellow accents. The bottom floors are dedicated to commerce—cafes, shoe stores, lamp boutiques, wine bars, art galleries, and coffee shops—the usual for a bustling European hub. Walking the hilly streets affords you a view of a castle with its arches and spires, where I imagined royalty surveying their land holdings all the way down to the river. A grand past whispered its mystery into the city's ambiance. Perhaps this castle wasn't exciting to Europeans, but to me—a child of a young nation where castles exist only in fairytales and Disneyworld—it held an allure.

The Portuguese are known for being the most relaxed Europeans. Maybe it's all that cobblestone, but they go at their own pace and pay no mind to yours. Is the restaurant you want to eat at full? The owner will come out and spend ten minutes recommending her favorite local spots and even call them to check if they have a table open before she sends you in that direction. One night, a lovely woman who ran a bustling restaurant called Tapabene recommended that we eat at her favorite local joint a few houses down, called Rapido. Real Portuguese food, skilled chefs, but "honest," she said. Perfect. Ted and I enjoyed a meal of olives, vegetable soup, *alheira* (Portuguese sausage), fish, and ox meat.

The energy around our table initially threw me off. We were seated smack in the middle of the dining room. Against a backdrop of pale-yellow walls, diners surrounded us like the numbers on an analog clock, tick-tocking with chatter in all directions. Restaurants can be tricky when you practice sensing the energy around you. There's no escape! It felt awkward and uncomfortable, and I had to concentrate on my conversation with Ted.

Once we got beyond the typical chit-chat of what to eat and what to do the next day, our attention naturally engaged and the noise of our surroundings disappeared. Somehow, we started talking about capital punishment, a random conversation for us as we don't usually spend much mental bandwidth on the topic, an American anomaly of social policy with which most of the West disagrees. Somehow, sitting in this Portuguese restaurant, the subject was on the table. For what may have been the first time as an adult, I seriously asked myself what I believed about capital punishment and couldn't come up with a satisfying answer. No revelation relieved me of my ambivalence. I simply saw too many perspectives about the issue to decide which one was better than any other.

Ted started with his perspective, a sturdy point of view that he had been building on for years. "There are so many levels to it," he began, always eager to lay the foundation for his opinion. (He excelled in law school.) "I don't think my position is grounded in the morality of it, but in the ineptness of the justice system. The unfairness of it. It's so obviously prejudiced, and I can't stand behind a system that so disproportionately impacts the black community."

That was a very Ted answer—well-conceived, rational, and applaudable. "And what's more," he went on, "we put innocent people to death. How many convicts on death row are later exonerated?" It was a rhetorical question as neither of us knew the exact number, but the fact that it's more than zero made it too large. "I can't support that," he concluded.

"I agree," I offered, nodding my head in a show of support. I did agree with his reasoning, but it seemed to touch only the edges of the issue. I couldn't put my finger on what that was yet, so I started talking and let my feelings guide my words. "I think my feelings about capital punishment have shifted beyond the failings of our government. I think even if we had a non-prejudicial judicial system that only put to death those who were guilty of some unanimously agreed upon atrocity like murder, I wouldn't want that."

"Sure, yeah," Ted shrugged, poking his fork at the fatty bits of ox meat left on his plate. "I don't think I would want to put anyone to death either. But don't do the crime if you can't do the time, you know? Everyone knows that the death penalty is a possibility for heinous crimes, so if you commit one you are basically consenting to the consequences. And if the family of the victim wanted it, needed it to move on with their lives, then I would defer to them."

"Why?" I asked, plopping my elbow on the table and resting my chin in my hand.

"Because it's justice. We must take people as they are now, and in our current reality some people need the death of a perpetrator to close a horrible chapter of their lives and move on."

I wondered out loud, "How do you know they need it?"

"They say they do." He eyed me warily, seeing I was going somewhere with this line of questioning. He's very smart, my husband. The thing is, I had no idea where I was going with it, but I have found that asking *why* is always useful for digging underneath things, and that's where I wanted to go.

"Look," he started. He likes to say "look" when he's about to stand on principle. "Look, I know we can't know. People may think they need a particular thing to move on and they have no idea whether it's really the closure they need or whether, once they get it, there will be another thing. But I want to honor their reality. Putting someone to death is one of the most serious decisions we can make, and if the victim's family arrives at a place where they feel comfortable making that decision, I want to honor it."

I understood but I couldn't agree. Maybe I did once; I honestly can't remember what I used to think. But I knew exactly what I thought sitting in that restaurant. "I love that you want to respect the families of the victims. It sounds like this is your way of showing empathy for their experience and not wanting to judge it. Which is a beautiful intention."

"But . . ." Ted said, circling his fork in the air motioning me to get on with it. He could feel my perspective building like a wave, about to crest over.

I chuckled and nodded. "But there's still something incomplete in that for me. There are so many perspectives about controversial issues like the death penalty. There are so many lenses through which we can examine the issue—contexts and nuances, history and politics, social psychology and philosophy, emotion and statistics. It's not about choosing which one holds more credibility; it's not about choosing any of them. They are all constructs."

"Okay, so what is underneath those constructs for you?" Ted asked.

I had been practicing seeing the world from the viewpoint of my inner wisdom, unencumbered by dogma. "Grace," I said, almost shrugging with its simplicity. "My soul does not judge. It is only the thinking mind that judges. From the perspective of our souls, there is only loving awareness of the world. The soul sees only the soul inside of everyone else and is rather unconcerned with what we say and do. When we can access our soul's perspective and recognize the soul in others, we see them as they truly are, animated from the same life force energy as we are. From here, grace flows. My soul embraces the soul it's being asked to judge and invites the person layered on top to recognize himself as a soul."

I felt Ted's ears prick up. He was following my philosophy and poised for the shoe to drop—the practical application. "But can we guarantee they won't kill another person?" *Boom.* Shoe dropped.

"Well, isn't justice about bringing balance back?" I threw out my palms as if they were the scales of justice. "Where is the balance if we are stacking more violence on the scale?"

"But it's potentially saving the life of another person."

"Potentially, that is true. But I think there is greater power in offering grace—giving the person a chance to find peace within himself. In recognizing ourselves for who we truly are, we find peace. Inner peace is a remarkable catalyst for change—how we show up in the world inevitably changes when how we feel about ourselves changes. What could be more powerful than inviting someone to love himself? To recognize that he is not broken? Which is exactly what we say when we condemn them to death."

"That sounds like a great future, but it's not the reality of how people are right now." So practical, my husband.

That's where we get stuck. Ted, along with most people I know, lend credibility to our current reality because it is true right now. (He would want me to say this has since changed for him.) I understand that what we are experiencing now is *what is*, and to ignore *what is* seems to be a form of denial, a way of living in the clouds.

Fortunately for us all, that is a misperception. What's true right now is only a product of the past. In the middle of a yellow-walled Portuguese home cookery, I realized that this conversation was not about the ethical dilemma of capital punishment, and it wasn't even about the perspective of the soul. The real gem wrapped inside the cloak of this conversation was seeing how we unconsciously create a future modeled on the past. It didn't matter what Ted's perspective was, or what I felt my soul's perspective was. It wasn't about thoughts and constructs and souls. It was about our power to create reality. We can create a reality that looks far different from how it does right now, much faster than we realize. Right now, in fact.

We give such deference to what we can see, smell, touch, taste, and hear, and call it "the way it is." But indeed, "the way it is" is nothing more than a snapshot of the past that made it so. Like driving a car, we must look straight through the windshield at what's ahead to navigate where we want to go. Looking sideways out the window to where we are now in hopes of getting where we want to go is a risky way to drive! As philosopher Jiddu Krishnamurti said, "It is no measure of health to be well adjusted to a profoundly sick society." To honor what is real right now is to enable it in perpetuity.

I put down my fork and looked up to the left, as I often do when I am searching for words to explain something I haven't mapped out yet. "You're right, the future I envision isn't the current reality of society. But how else can I influence the future but to stand for what I know it can be?" And why shouldn't I? We love the stories of inventors and scientists and engineers who beat the odds and the naysaying of their critics in pursuit of their life's work, finally bringing forth a great gift that propels humanity forward. These stories inspire us to live in our truth, even if no one else understands it or supports it. Who knows what may come of it?

I was reminded of a great line by Rabbi Hillel in the Talmud, a book of Jewish commentary compiled by distinguished rabbis throughout the ages. They converse and argue with each other over interpretations of the Torah, each leaving their wisdom to chew on by the next rabbi who comes along, often centuries later. The line is simply, "If not now, when?" All the American Jews I grew up with know this line, which is part of a larger paragraph that urges us to speak and act on our truth now. Once we claim our truth, how can we sit and wait? How can we deny it?

The time is *now* to claim our power as the creators of reality. This is the ultimate leadership role. We are not beholden to whatever we've already created. Whatever we've done, whatever we've chosen, whatever we've built with our lives thus far has so much momentum behind it that it can seem impossible to change. We can *feel* powerless to make a different choice, but the truth is that we are never powerless. We can always claim our truth and do something about it. It might be small and slow, or huge and swift. Either way, it's always in our power whether we lean into our life's momentum or choose what we truly desire. One day, we will have both.

There is immense power in claiming our truth, and this is all we need to do to transform into the leaders of our lives. Don't wait for what you think and how you feel to be acceptable to society, to your mom, to your lover. Don't be rational about it, don't compromise it for something more palatable. No one else is living your life.

The power comes when *we* accept what we want for ourselves. This simple act of acceptance shifts us into integrity with our true self and creates space to hear our Voice clearly. When we follow the wisdom of our truth, we use our energy efficiently. It takes so much energy to be inauthentic, to constantly wonder if what we believe, say, or do is the right thing. Once we own our truth, we get to be who we are, and we can funnel our energy to do something about it.

MILESTONES

INNER GUIDANCE

> The present moment is a snapshot of the thinking and doing of the past that made it so.

- We unconsciously tend to create the future based on our blueprint of the past. To create a different future, we must let go of our attachment to *what is*.
- Instead, look to what we *want* to create. Owning the truth of what we want is something we can do right now. We don't need to wait for anyone to give us permission or make it acceptable.
- The power in creating the reality we want comes when we stand up for it, even silently in our own minds.
- When we accept our truth, we step into the energy of leadership and become the masters of our destiny.

DEEPER NAVIGATION

1. Take some time to reflect on your top five values in life. These could be related to family, career, health, recreation, spirituality, or something else. How would you feel if each value were real and true right now? Feel it in your heart and in your body. Notice what emotions come up.
2. What is one thing you can do right now to support one of your top five values? It doesn't need to be huge or fast, but it needs to be an action.
3. What is leadership to you? In what areas of life do you take action on what you want? In what areas are you in observation mode?

18

I AM INFINITE

Ohm's footprints (2019)

My intention is to tell
of bodies changed
to different forms . . .
The heavens and all below them,
Earth and her creatures,
All change,
And we, part of creation,
Also must suffer change.
—Ovid, *Metamorphoses*

I could have never imagined this. Yes, I craved expansion, connection, liberation, and courage, but I hadn't asked for *this*—an experience that stretched my understanding of reality to the brink. In the silence of winter 2019, I had a daughter, and then I didn't. I wove together flesh and blood, and then I said goodbye to my creation, my little girl. Now I have a paper heart stamped with two impossibly tiny feet, each with five little toes no larger than chia seeds. Hanging on my wall, this heart reminds me of how we transformed together, and how I'll never be the same.

I had never been one of those women who felt the inevitability of motherhood. My eyes were on the prize of my career, and while I certainly believed that I could have it all if I wanted, I wasn't convinced I wanted children. Growing up, my relationship with my mother was strained and I took the responsibility of motherhood quite seriously. I wasn't sure if I was up for the challenge of guiding another human through the world.

Most of the men I dated wanted children, which put me in a bit of a quandary. Was I committed to not having children or was there wiggle room? The best I could do was say I was agnostic about parenthood, as there was certainly a piece of me that *wished* I wanted to be a mother because it seemed it would make the dating game much easier. Also, something about men wanting children resonated much more deeply with me than women wanting children. I rolled my eyes when my girlfriends talked about becoming parents one day, believing that they were brainwashed. That same societal imprinting didn't apply to men in my mind, so when they started smiling as they talked about becoming dads, I wanted to dive inside their minds and see what inspired their smile. Maybe it could inspire one for me, too.

After years of tinkering with my perspective on motherhood, it transformed from an arduous obligation of biology to a magical expression of love and creativity. Simply, my own journey towards motherhood no longer felt attached to my experience of childhood. I felt an incredible excitement about what I could offer the child who would choose me as its mom. All the love I had inside welled up and I started chasing Ted around the bedroom to turn us into parents. Each breath was joined by a wish to start our family.

Before we left on our next adventure, we found an OB-GYN and took care of the responsibilities of future parents-to-be. As Jews, there are some genetic mutations in our lineage to watch out for, so we took blood tests to be sure that we were in the clear. Unfortunately, we weren't. We immediately called our doctor, who explained the genetic disorder we both carried known as PKU (phenylketonuria), and its impact on a child and the family.

I was in shock. The doctor's voice sounded like the teacher from "Peanuts," just a tinny and unintelligible "wah wah wah" through the phone. The power of denial rushed forward to my defense. I wondered if this news would go away if I hung up the phone or rolled it up like a carpet that I could shove in the back of a closet. If I could rewind my day by ten minutes, maybe I could look at the blood test results again and they would be different.

Our doctor counseled us to see a genetic specialist and a fertility specialist regarding our options for conception and to learn about IVF (In Vitro Fertilization), a pricey process that screens your reproductive material before implantation. She recommended we stop trying to conceive naturally until we had a chance to speak with these experts, who would help us make a more informed decision about what to do. My stomach twisted.

Suddenly our bedroom was full of people who didn't belong there. Specialists, doctors, nurses, lab technicians, pharmacies, online mom groups, and I could only imagine who else was now going to be part of my path to conception. I felt exposed and guilty. I wasn't sure of what, but I felt like I had failed at something. I had not wanted children for so long, feeling they were unnecessary—an obstacle even—to accomplish my personal dreams. I was adamant that I had evolved past my biological drive to prioritize procreation. And then I went through this journey of self-discovery, lit my energy on fire, and surprisingly only to me, my desire shifted. Now I wanted nothing more than to create life. It became central to my dharma that I birth the next generation of awakened souls, guiding them into this world through my womb.

Parenthood felt so natural, the most natural thing in the world. Now the purity of my desire felt stained. This woman in a lab coat reading from a chart was telling me to STOP? Ted and I were about to hop on a plane, so these new doctors would have to wait. But I didn't want to wait. The drive to become a parent had come so fast and so strong it seemed to be carrying me forward with a life of its own. I didn't feel capable of waiting. We had a 75% chance of conceiving a perfectly healthy baby, potentially making all of this a nonissue.

Ted and I arrived in Morocco to attend the first personal development retreat of its kind, called Vortex Global Leadership Transformation. Its mission is to invite global leaders to practice leading from the heart, believing that a world whose leaders operate from a place of love, compassion, and service is one in which humanity can thrive. On the plane to Marrakech, I leaned over and whispered to Ted that I was four days late. Our eyes met and I watched him light up with the first smile of a father-to-be. He held my hand and shut his eyes, leaning back into his seat. We quietly held hands for the rest of the flight. I calculated the possibility of getting my hands on a pregnancy test in the mountains of Morocco, which was slim to none.

L'Amandier is a beautiful resort nestled in the Atlas Mountains an hour south of Marrakech. Built on a natural bed of crystals, it is infused with tranquil energy. So there we were in Morocco, with the reality of our predicament fully in our laps—and growing in mine. Each day we would wake up in our plush, oversized bedroom, and I'd go to the bathroom to confirm I had not gotten my period. Ted would wrap me in a big hug and we'd smile, telling ourselves this was meant to be. I was in love with this little life, my heart already expanding into motherhood. Nestled in the grandness of the mountains in an oasis of pomegranate trees and rose bushes, pregnant with a child that I so deeply wanted, I was floating in bliss. I could have lived in that moment forever.

Our last night at L'Amandier was something of a celebration, a special dinner followed by dancing. To my surprise, one of the lead facilitators of the self-development program, Howard, led us in a beautiful ceremony to celebrate the new little life growing in my belly. The room glowed with soft candlelight. Voices joined together in song as the women lifted me up and the men carried Ted, sprinkling rose petals over us. Exalted by our new Moroccan tribe, Ted and I surrendered to this blessing over this miraculous moment.

Howard is Jewish, although I don't know if he would describe himself that way. He is a student of many religions and embraces them all with incredible respect. Ted and I had both dived headfirst into the nondogmatic waters of spirituality, leaving Judaism at its shores. I wasn't sure how Judaism fit into my life at that point, if at all. How could there be room for religion and all its rules in my new framework of Oneness? I had shelved Judaism, rejecting its dogma. Any "musts," "shoulds," and "laws" of religion struck me as false, man-made, and unrelated to connecting with "God." I had learned that the divine doesn't require us to jump through hoops. There are no sacrifices that must be made, promises that must be kept, or foods that cannot be eaten.

We expected that Howard might offer a generic spiritual blessing about reincarnation and the *bardos*, wise words from Rumi, or wax poetic on the cosmos. Instead, he recited a straightforward, formal Hebrew prayer used for centuries, if not millennia, for the express purpose of blessing the family formed by a new pregnancy. I burst into tears. Somehow, hearing the words of my ancestral faith lit up a space deep within me that I hadn't been in touch with for a long time, if ever.

Judaism came alive for me in a way I had never experienced when I recited Hebrew prayers in Sunday school. I could no longer deny I was Jewish as my body responded to Howard's prayer, completely collapsing the wall I had built between religion and spirituality. As tears streamed down my face, it was viscerally apparent that I could be simultaneously Jewish and spiritual, and it no longer needed to make sense. My body knew what my mind did not, and its reaction to Howard's blessing broke the dam that had been holding back the power of Judaism from flooding my heart. In a great pouring in of love, my resistance to religion was swept away.

In Judaism, family is the wheel of life. It is the family that carries the covenant between people and God: that God watches over and protects us as long as we have faith. To me, all that this means is that in order to experience the awesome power of the Universe, you have to be open to it. As a mother-to-be, I had the privilege of stepping into the wheel of life to honor my child with the grace of God. To offer her the Universe.

With this pregnancy I was no longer alone, doing life on my own. I was no longer suspended in space and time but connected forwards and backwards to the people whose lives turned the wheel over and over. I was connected to the divinity of their experiences, their love, their pain, their stories. Their lives carved the shape of my own. This little one inside me was now a part of this great wheel and together we moved it forward.

Without a little blue stick to hold onto, this blessing made the pregnancy real. Of course, as soon as we left Morocco, I used a pregnancy test and watched the blue plus sign grow bold. Ted made an appointment with a perinatal doctor who would conduct the genetic test on our baby when we arrived back in the States. The test couldn't be done until the twelfth week of pregnancy, so we enjoyed our weeks of ignorance in bliss.

My connection to the growing life within grew stronger every day. I loved this baby in a way that I hadn't ever loved anything in the world. I understood why my mother said loving a child is unlike any other love. I felt the energy and vitality of this baby differently from everything else. When I started waking up at 4 a.m. ferociously nauseous and simultaneously ravenous, I thought, *life is perfect.*

We gave our baby the nickname Ohm, the symbol for universal creation. I was creating a universe inside me. We decided to put our backpacks down and purchased a home in Austin, Texas. We imagined our baby growing up there, chasing the lizards in the backyard and trick-or-treating in the neighborhood. Through exhaustion, nausea, and moving across the globe, our hearts exploded into parenthood.

Pregnancy forged the most intense connection to life that I had ever known, and I experienced unparalleled joy as I welcomed the child borne of Ted's and my love. Magic of new life unfolded within the universe of my body. New cells moved and divided and became. Blood ran between us. Love ran between us. What was mine was hers and hers was mine. Wherever I was, there she was. Wherever she was, there I was too.

This constant, undeniable connection to the miracle of life offered me deeper access to its intelligence. My intuition heightened; my perspective widened. The need to run my Voice by my brain for validation disappeared. I had completely surrendered to the *knowing*. Divinity was sourced straight from my womb, from the spirit of the child that was settling into her new home inside the body we were building for her.

How much fuller I felt with this precious one. I glowed every minute. We communicated with each other through our connection—I was her cradle and she was my power. The force of life is overpowering. She was me and I was her, and I couldn't remember what it was like to not be pregnant. I felt sorry for Ted for drawing the short stick of being a man, unable to experience this magic.

At our perinatal appointment in Austin, the doctor said results would come in about ten to fourteen days, which put us at fifteen weeks and Christmas time. I was excited to be able to share the joy of our news with everyone during the holidays. Ted's family planned annual Christmas trips together and this year we were going to Ojai, California. On Christmas Day we arrived in Ojai and Ted's family cooed over my growing belly. We talked about the baby's due date in June, squealed over tiny socks, and swapped stories of our own childhoods.

By December 26th, we were antsy. We hadn't received a call from the doctor's office and didn't want to get lost in the Christmas shuffle. When I woke up that morning in the hotel, it was the first thing on my mind. As if on cue, my phone rang. I didn't recognize the number and picked it up innocently as I strode across the room to put on clothes.

"This is Texas Perinatal Group. Can I speak with Danielle Sunberg?"

I froze. I glanced over at Ted who was lying in bed playing on his phone. "This is Danielle."

"I have the results from your genetic test."

"Okay, great. Thanks for calling. Go ahead." I swallowed my anticipation.

"The fetus inherited the genetic abnormality from both parents."

"What?" A one-word plea for a different answer.

"The fetus inherited the gene mutation from both parents."

Silence.

"Oh," I said after a few moments to acknowledge that I was still on the phone. I looked at Ted. I couldn't tell if he was aware of what was going on. My head was spinning; I couldn't work out how to put the phone on speaker so he could hear.

"So," I mustered up the courage to say something, "the baby isn't healthy?" Saying it out loud on my side of the conversation, Ted understood what was happening and put his phone down to look at me. I stared back at him like a deer in headlights.

"Right."

"Can you tell me the gender?" When they do the genetic test, they also learn the gender, and I wanted to know everything I could about the little life I was carrying.

"Your baby is a girl," the nurse said. She relayed all this news so matter-of-factly. It was hard to believe there was a human on the other side of this phone call.

"Oh, okay, thanks," I said. *What was I thanking her for*, I wondered? The nurse said she would send the medical records over to my doctor and I was welcome to call her to discuss anything further. I hung up the phone and sat down on the bed.

Ted and I sat silently together, unsure of what to say. I was terribly afraid of saying or doing anything. If I sat perfectly still, maybe life would stop moving forward. For the second time I wished to rewind time to before I answered the phone. What happened next is blurry. I don't remember what we said or what we did, except that we stayed in bed and shut out the world for a long time. We must have told both of our parents, but I don't remember how it happened. We wanted to lock our thoughts in a safe and forget the combination, so we turned on the TV and ordered overpriced hotel movies until sleep mercifully found us.

There is a moment when dreams slip into reality. I nuzzled into the soft pillow and felt the warmth of morning sun streaming onto my face. Not yet awake, I shifted on the bed to readjust, ready to curl up into my dreams. And then my mind stirred, noticed the bed wasn't my own, and remembered I was at a hotel. All at once I remembered I was in California, and if I was in California then I would also remember . . . wait, I wouldn't let my mind finish that thought. Wait. Hold perfectly still and maybe the dreams will take me away again and I will wake up in a different reality. A tear rolled out of my still closed eyes. I couldn't stop remembering.

The morning was a blur of hiding from reality and giving myself an inner pep talk. I could accept this. I *must* accept this so that I could move forward. Decisions needed to be made, plans needed to be changed, and I needed to envision a different future that still looked bright enough to walk towards. I needed air. Ted and I wandered outside and took a seat in the Adirondack chairs circling a fire pit with a view of the Ojai mountains. We held hands and quietly watched the sun creep upwards above the peaks, a stinging reminder that life moves forward, no matter what. After letting silence hang in the air, it was time to say what needed to be said.

"What are we going to do?" I asked.

Ted shrugged his shoulders and exhaled. "I don't know."

I looked out onto the horizon beyond the mountain peaks where the universe hid its secrets. I knew the answer to my own question and I knew Ted did, too, but saying it out loud felt too real.

Looking away from Ted, I said, "We need to fly home and take care of this, of ourselves." Tears streamed down my face, running over my cheeks in big fat drops.

"I know," Ted said, nodding along. "Are you sure?" he asked.

"It's not what I want to do, but it's what we are going to do." What I wanted to do was turn back time, change reality, make Ohm healthy. But as I couldn't afford to spend time in denial, I needed to make a choice. We were going to terminate this pregnancy. I had already gone down the research rabbit hole of what quality of life this rare genetic disorder offered to the child and the parents.

I felt the weight of playing God. The questions that arose during my private decision-making process rocked me to the core. *Who was I to make this decision? Who was I to guard the gates of life? What did my decision mean about myself? Was I a bad person?*

It was as though the entire journey I had been on, the countries I had visited and the insights I had awoken to since quitting the law firm were all preparation to equip me with the tools I needed to navigate the dilemma I now faced. I recognized the futility of trying to answer any of the questions rattling around in my brain. There were no answers; there was only perspective, as transient as the sun in the sky. Ultimately, the decision was clear, and I knew what Ted and I faced next at a family clinic. As we sat in our Adirondack chairs looking out at the majesty of nature, we contemplated the volatility and horror that could come with it. I continued to sit quietly and focused on breathing in acceptance of what was and what was to be.

I felt a shift. Ohm had been present with me everywhere I went. The duality of mother and child had collapsed into Oneness, and she was both the embodiment of divinity and my connection to it. Now, accepting that this pregnancy was about to end and that this child growing inside of me would never be born seemed to sever our connection. In one breath I no longer felt her flowing within me. She disappeared. In that moment, I no longer felt pregnant. I felt like only me, alone in my body. The power of the divine was gone. I felt small and alone. I put my hand over my stomach as I turned to Ted and whispered, "She's gone." Tears rolled down my cheeks. I didn't even get to say goodbye, and now I couldn't feel her anymore.

Ted, my darling intuitive husband, waited for me to climb out of my grief and meet his gaze. When I looked up at him with desperation, he squeezed my hand and said, "She's not gone. We agreed together, the three of us, that it was time, so she left. But she is here," he concluded as he waved his hand in the space around us. "I feel her," he whispered.

A wave of emotions crested over, feelings of heartache and relief, pain and joy, as I recognized this truth. I felt it reverberate through my body, burn through my bones, and settle sweetly in my heart. Oh, how much peace his words bring me still! She never left. She simply changed forms.

On the most visceral level, I experienced that we are not our bodies. I didn't understand it, but I lived it. The spark that gives us our *us-ness* has nothing to do with our bones, skin, and teeth. I had sensed my baby's spirit leave her own body from inside my body. I felt the weight of emptiness, even while her body's little heart beat and her legs kicked, she was no longer there.

It was a strange thing to experience a soul come into my body and then leave it. Stranger still to be the sole consciousness to experience it. As much as Ted went through this journey beside me, he was not inside my womb. He could not—no one could—participate in the physical unfolding of this cosmic experience. But he felt it in his own way. He felt her soul envelop him like a comforting blanket. A man who feels most assured when he can hold his experiences like dirt in his hands, Ted experienced the life of our child with as much unyielding certainty as the solid ground under his feet.

Creating Ohm catapulted me into the realm of motherhood with awesome force, and I had no idea how to hold onto this expansion without holding a baby in my arms. Everything surged through me: joy, pain, suffering, love, fear, gratitude, anger, confusion, jealousy, desperation, appreciation, curiosity, denial, compassion, acceptance. They didn't wait their turn or stand in line so I could feel them one by one. No, they flooded in all at once, drowning any story that could possibly make sense of this and keep me afloat. With nothing to cling to, I gulped for air, panicking that I'd never find solid ground again. I kicked and thrashed as the water continued to pour over me.

I ached for her, my eyes straining over my feelings to see someone who wasn't there. My legs constantly churned water as I bobbed up and down, peering out onto the empty horizon. I held onto her in the form of denial. To stop searching for her was to drown. Every time the waves pulled me under, I caught a glimpse of surrender and fought my way back up to the surface. I wore myself out, the way we tend to do with grief. On the outside I smiled at the grocery store clerk, waved to my neighbors when I got the mail, and met friends for coffee. On the inside I kicked and thrashed.

Until I stopped. I didn't want to hold onto her this way anymore. I stopped fighting to stay above the surface of my grief and surrendered to the ocean. Down, down, down I sank until daylight couldn't find me. Down, down, down I descended through the darkness. Down, down, down I went until one day my endless journey of sinking stopped. The bottom of the sea. Cradled by the seabed and a tender solidness I thought I had forever abandoned, I opened my eyes and looked around. The depths of the water had washed away the yearning that clouded my sight. With clear eyes, I saw all there was to see: the ocean. The ocean of motherhood, a place endlessly expansive and completely private to Ohm and to me. It was our ocean. She was here with me. I couldn't be here without her. What I saw clearly was that I hadn't lost Ohm at all. I only needed to look somewhere else.

In becoming a mother, I experienced the cycle of the non-physical becoming physical and recycling back into the non-physical. I felt the mysterious transformation of *being* within the universe of my body. Tuning into this experience illuminated the most profound wisdom I've yet remembered. *We are not our bodies.* The thunderous, deafening, incredible power of who we are is infinite.

Through all my self-exploration I had come to understand that *we are not our minds*, and that was . . . mind blowing. Somehow, I hadn't yet connected the dots that we are also not our bodies. Who we are transcends our bones and kidneys and eyebrows. We are everything, we are everywhere, we are always. I am still her, and she is still me. Our lives and loves are intertwined. Now. Then. Here. There. Especially there.

This was the salvation that offered me peace. In this quiet place at the bottom of the sea there was still suffering and joy, but I had become the ocean holding it all. I was the moon, the stars, the tide, and the seaweed. In this quiet place, I saw how I could live with all of it: I will always find her when I look clearly. This remains constant and true no matter the weather and it invited me back to myself. I had no idea how to pick up my tattered pieces off the ground and sew them back together. Who I had become in the aftermath of releasing Ohm back to the universe didn't need those pieces any longer. I was to create myself anew. All the "I ams" that had settled into my bones came together to forge a new version of me.

I am the Mother of all creation.

As I started to sew this truth into the fabric of my being, I realized I would never be done. There was no end to the impact of forever and everywhere. I had witnessed life's infinity through plants, Ted, a dead brother, my own daughter, and ultimately, myself. That we are infinitely more than our bodies means that we are not playing a finite game that we lose when we die. We live on in different shapes, never gone, only transformed. We are playing an infinite game in which death is simply a roll of the dice that catapults us to another phase of the game.

When I saw that life is infinite, I could play with it differently. Life, death, and the bridge we walk between them have no rules, at least not the ones we think. When I surrendered what I thought I knew about life and death, I started playing this infinite game and peace found me. Ohm is still here, and we are still playing together. I know it because I feel her tenderness envelope me when I call for her. We communicate with each other in much the same way we did before.

I had been swallowed whole by wondering if *I* had taken Ohm's life away. It tore me up and ripped me apart to think that I could create and destroy this child. I wanted nothing more than to keep her. But what I felt that day sitting in the Adirondack chairs was that I had nothing to do with death. Ohm left upon our family's agreement, one she quite insisted upon. She left her body because she chose to. It was my holy and venerated duty to clean up the physical remains of that agreement.

Experiencing life's infinity can offer a deep well of serenity. If we do not die, then we cannot kill—not in the way we so fear. We never truly take another's "life" because the spirit does not end when the body ceases to breathe. We cannot take away our *is-ness*. Our spark of sentience carries on in its new way of being. Our intelligence holds no grudges, feels no fear, and carries no resentment. When it leaves the body, it does not *mind* what happens to the body. In this knowing, there is an infinite well of peace.

And as the inner is a mirror of the outer, life's infinity reoriented me to see peace on the cosmic scale. In a world that on the whole has agreed to play a finite game, death becomes negative, abhorrent, feared. We value our ability to play the game above all else, and we are distraught over the end of another's ability to play. We wail over untimely deaths caused by single actors and countries alike. In war there is much ending of game play; when we think in times of peace, there is not.

Does peace arrive only when there is no more death? That doesn't set us up very well if we are going to keep dying. Peace is already here. It was always here and it has never left. In the same way as individuals are not broken, death does not break us or end us. Our wholeness thrives on the ultimate scale of humanity. There is nothing bad or wrong or splintered about death. It is, for now, inevitable. However, death is only one change in the game. Our spirits remain completely whole, safe, and well as they move on to a new phase. When we understand the cosmic nature of life and we start to play an infinite game, we might not only find peace within ourselves, but also across the whole world.

Life is infinite settled into my bones. Serene and sober, I stepped out of the ocean and onto dry shores. I experienced the cycle of life and death from the inside out. The glory of creation and the violence of destruction blew me apart. I navigated every emotion that humans are capable of feeling, dialed up to the max. And when I finally turned around on the beach to gaze back at the sparkling sea, I felt her. Ohm never left me, really. She is still here beside me, around me, through me. She is a wide ocean of love and patience that brings me back to the grounding force of infinity.

MILESTONES

INNER GUIDANCE

> ↢ There is great wisdom in suffering and hardship. They can lead to some of life's most astonishing insights.

> ↢ We are more than our bodies. Our bodies are a vehicle for experiencing life.

> ↢ We are infinite, our intelligence unlimited by space and time.

> ↢ The finality of death is an illusion. When our bodies die, we live on. The way we experience life transforms into our next phase of being, and we remain whole and well.

> ↢ Consequently, there is peace on earth available to us right now.

DEEPER NAVIGATION

1. Reflect on some things you have let go of in the last year. These can be big or small, like ending a job or tossing out old clothes. What has emerged in the space you created by letting go?

2. Suffering and hardship can lead to some of our biggest insights in life. Reflect on any insights you've gained through an experience of great hardship. How have these insights influenced you? What would it look like to integrate them more fully into your life?

3. Take some time to reflect on your relationship to death. What does death mean to you? How do you feel about death? Your relationship to death directly impacts your relationship to life and how you live in each moment. What do you notice?

4. Take some time to reflect on the legacy you will leave when you pass on. What is the impact that you hope to have made? What will you be most proud of? Remember, even the smallest moments can have huge consequences.

19

I AM POSSIBLE

Danielle writing this book in Santa Fe, New Mexico (2019)

Stepping out of my ocean of grief, I heeded the call to dry out in the American Southwest, with its sun-drenched mesas and saguaro cacti. I wanted to be where the arid canyons and dusty skies honored the pure and ancient Mother. Santa Fe embraced my adventure, and Ted and I planned to spend a long afternoon wandering the psychonaut's funhouse called Meow Wolf.

Meow Wolf is a trip through seventy rooms of interactive art, and I can't recommend the ride enough. In our third hour of walking around this magical, mystical, reality warp, we came to a room decorated in mind-bending, black-and-white illusions of depth perception. As I traced the geometry with my eyes and felt my body pulled and pushed by tricks of design, I caught the subtle outline of a doorway. My hand tingled with the excitement as I turned the knob and opened this secret passageway. I expected a crazy, colorful, topsy-turvy experience to greet me. Instead, I found myself walking into a dim chamber, quiet and peaceful. Its stoic plainness resembled a chapel. A hard rectangular bench lined the walls. There was nothing to do but sit.

Part of me thought, "Oh, boring. This must be the room for people who need a break from the trip. Let's move on." Another part of me laughed at my knee-jerk need for constant stimulation. I'd trusted everything this place offered me up to now, so why not lean into whatever this room had in store? I chose a spot on the bench far enough away from the three other people quietly sitting in the room so that my experience wouldn't merge into theirs. Ted sat next to me and we started to meditate. We had come to love meditating in new places, letting the energy of the space infuse the vibration of our transcendence.

After a few cleansing breaths, an intention bubbled up. I heard myself ask for a new spiritual guide to step forward—one I hadn't met before—with whom I could resonate as I was about to become a mother. Ted and I had moved forward quickly with IVF and conceived another child, a daughter we would name Rhea, who was rapidly taking up room in my belly. I let myself fall back into meditation. Or rather, I tried. A memory swirled into my mind, some unimportant childhood memory with my mom. I swatted at the distraction getting in the way of channeling this new guide.

Then suddenly I stopped myself. A rather novel and interesting thought popped into my head. "Could my *mom* be the guide stepping forward?" The higher version of her, the spiritual essence that tran-scends the body? (She was very much alive and likely sitting comfortably on her couch at that very moment.) Curiously, I asked, "Mom, are *you* my guide?"

"Of course," I heard. "I've always been your guide," my mom's Voice whispered to me. "You've held me at arms' length your entire life, and now you are ready to receive me." She appeared in my mind's eye, taking shape as a big crystal, clear and shining brightly with facets of light refracting throughout her creating dazzling rainbows. I followed her stream of light across the sky to a smaller crystal that I recognized as myself. A rainbow of her light flowed into my own crystalline body that bent it, shaped it, and sent it back out to the universe as a completely new beam of light. Through her light, I had shaped my own.

I was a prism for my mother's light, receiving her brilliance and shining it my own way. It was the purest interpretation of what I could offer my future children, something I had started to think about as I grew rounder. The image clarified a thousand things I had wondered, even as a fully grown adult. *What does it mean to be nurtured by parents and then grow up to become your own person? Can you learn their values and be free to make your own choices? Can you turn away from what they want for you while simultaneously offering gratitude? Can you reflect without copying?*

Overpowered by the guidance I had received, I opened my eyes for a few moments, returning from the twilight zone of a crystalline sky to this quiet chamber tucked away inside a raucous art house. I closed my eyes again and felt for her, hoping the connection wasn't severed. She appeared immediately. Of course she did; she's my mom. She told me that it was her time to be my guide because *I* decided she could be. The thought had never occurred to me that my mother could be a spiritual teacher. Guides are sacred and special—gurus and saints, aliens and angels—and she was my *mom*.

"How could I step in to be your guide if you never gave me the room?" she asked. Giving a moment's curiosity to the thought "Oh, could my mom be my guide?" had offered her the possibility of stepping in. One thought, which took but a flicker of an instant, shifted my perspective that she *could be*, and so she became. It was like waving a magic wand that showed me a door I had never noticed before (not unlike the door to this chapel). Now that I had seen the door, I could open it and explore a whole new paradigm.

Common knowledge is that we must "see it to believe it," but this is completely backwards. We must believe in order to see. This became readily apparent when I reflected on the power of thoughts and realized that thoughts are the true creative force of life. We decide the limits of our reality through our beliefs, then reality expands and contracts around those limits. The lens through which we perceive the world is shaped by our beliefs. Even though many of them are unconscious, they shape and refract the light that comes into view.

I never understood that I had the option to choose the things that I believed. They were mostly handed down to me, imposed on me, and I didn't realize I had agency in the matter. No one in a position of authority said: "What I'm saying may not be true. It's up to you to decide for yourself." They simply taught me that *this is the way it is.* Good girls tell the truth. Bad boys fight. God is a judge. Be thin to be liked. Work hard to be successful.

Imagine keeping your head perfectly straight ahead for your whole life, and all you can see is a square. "It's a square," you say. You *know* it's a square. It's been a square your whole life. For years the square doesn't move or change. Then the earth jostles you enough to shift your neck slightly. With this new angle, the square suddenly becomes a cube. After a lifetime of seeing only a square, you now must contend with more dimensions, shades, aspects, and angles than you ever imagined existed.

We may refuse to consider evidence contrary to our world view and simply deny it. *There is no cube, only a square,* we say as we crane our necks back into position to see a square. Changing our belief systems can be completely disruptive to our lives. It's often too scary or overwhelming to consider that what we believed to be a rock-solid foundation isn't the whole truth. We built our lives and made serious choices based on the truth of a square—religions, rituals, marriages, and wars—and finding out that the square is not the whole truth can be too much to deal with. How foolish to sacrifice and pray and marry and fight if it's not based on truth! We contort ourselves, however uncomfortably, unwilling to acknowledge that we even saw the cube at all.

I'll assume that you are curious about seeing new shapes and can't help but marvel at the mysterious unknown. Once we allow ourselves to acknowledge that there is a cube, we also understand that this cube is not the end. Riding subtly underneath the discovery of the cube, like a barnacle on a whale, is the understanding that new shapes (and new doors) will continue to appear for the rest of our lives. This is the commitment of taking the red pill. Once we let go of the requirement for a belief to remain static and allow for the possibility that it can change, it inevitably will. A new door can appear and, even if we don't walk through it, its appearance is enough to alter our lives. To experience one flicker of curiosity about something we had never considered can shift our reality forever.

Sensing all the doors that I had yet to see, let alone open, left me reeling. Everything that I thought *was* became *maybe*. The solid ground beneath my feet disappeared and I was left staring into the vast cosmos of possibility. I found this quite overwhelming and disorienting, until I remembered that the floor was the illusion, and the unlimited nature of reality was the security of truth. What seemed like the emptiness I would fall through if I let go of the bench I sat on was really a cozy safety net prepared by the universe to catch me. Every door I had noticed so far was one I was grateful to have opened. Overwhelm transformed into overflowing gratitude.

Humbled by possibility, a new term for my life appeared: *adventure*. I had traveled over fourteen countries over six continents, but now I knew that the greatest adventure was inside. I would constantly find the edge of life and peer over it at the mystery that lay beyond. Looking past the rainbows cast by my mother was a deep blue ocean. I engulfed it hungrily and happily, the many-sided crystal of my body transforming into a mobius strip. In that moment I was free. My dimensions ever changing, fluid, formless. I was wild, unbottled, everywhere and in every way. I was off the well-worn path of personality. My body vibrated with knowing. *I am whole. I am safe. I am infinite.*

When I opened my eyes, I understood what knowing all of this made possible. When we know who we truly are, we don't only remember that we live on an infinite scale, but also that there are an infinite number of possibilities available to us. There are an infinite number of doors we can open. All of them are within our reach. All of them are safe. All of them offer adventure. All of them offer a chance to connect with our power. All of them will stretch us. All of them are worth walking through, but none of them need to be. It's up to us to decide where to go, and at what pace. It's up to us to pick our feet up off the ground, one by one, and move in the direction of our lives.

MILESTONES

INNER GUIDANCE

- Thoughts create our reality.
- What we believe is not set in stone. When we give ourselves permission to think something new, we create new possibilities for ourselves.
- Sometimes a new possibility can feel overwhelming and too scary to entertain. It's a new door we see but we are not ready to open it. That's okay! The fact that it exists can be incredibly powerful.
- Once we notice how our perspective shifts, it will continue to shift. This perpetual shift in perspective offers us a much different place to anchor ourselves.
- When everything is allowed to change, we can more easily enjoy opening the doors of expanded perspective.

DEEPER NAVIGATION

1. What messages about the world come from family, teachers, colleagues, media, religion, politics, advertisements, and sports? Have you denied yourself anything because it did not fit with these messages?
2. Think about your beliefs that have changed over time, maybe even over the course of this book. Write yourself a letter from twenty years in the future sharing the things you believe. What's changed?
3. Write a scene from a sci-fi movie in which you change one aspect of life. It could be time, space, color, smells, or a world with talking jellyfish. Let your imagination run wild. There are no rules.

20

I AM READY

Danielle, Ted, Rhea, and Ari (2022)

Fast forward a few years and I have given birth to my daughter Rhea and my son Ari. Ted and my toothbrushes no longer reside in a wad of tissue paper shoved into our backpacks but have their own dedicated cups in a bathroom of our house in Austin. I remember how excited Ted was to go grocery shopping and buy two cans of tomato sauce, knowing he could put away the extra can in our cupboard for another time.

Our lives transformed into something seemingly typical. A married couple with two children putting down roots. A truckload of boxes containing who we used to be arrived from D.C. I fluffed my squished throw pillows and plugged in my Nespresso machine, wondering if I was recreating my past. *Would my table lamp and my NutriBullet send me spiraling back to an outdated version of myself? Could the new me co-exist with old dishes?*

I was really asking, *is my transformation here to stay?* I sat on my couch hugging my fluffed pillow and wondered. Actually, I worried. I shook up my water bottle, which transported me into the past and carried that version of me into the future. I squeezed my pillow tighter.

"Try a different question," my Voice offered. It wasn't the answer that was problematic, it was the question.

In the morning I got out of bed and padded over to my bathroom to stare in the mirror. I tried a different question. "Who am I?" Suddenly I was back in my D.C. apartment leaning over the sink and peering into my eyes for the first time. It was the same question I had asked all that time ago, but this time was different. This time the answer was easy. My face was the same, my cheeks a little tanner and my hair a lot longer, but my eyes were different. My eyes weren't afraid to look. They stared back at me, calm and steady. They weren't scared of who they might find staring back at them.

Every day I look at my reflection and peer into my eyes to say, "*Hi.*" This is my spiritual practice. This is how I witness myself. This is me, honoring me. It doesn't matter who I find in the mirror, only that I am here for whoever she is. *I will not desert you.* It doesn't matter whether I am wearing a milk-stained sweatshirt or a pressed blouse (maybe even from Ann Taylor). It doesn't matter whether I am excited for the day or exhausted from the day, whether I am motivated to start my day or confused about where to start. None of it matters. What matters is that I meet my gaze. What matters is that whoever I find in the reflection is just fine. And if I want to change, then I'll change. Now I know how.

What doesn't change is that the woman I see in the mirror is connected to her life. Whether I am sitting with a client, watching her awaken to her own inner wisdom, or talking to Ted about a psychedelics company about to go public on the Nasdaq, I am filled with *life*. Whether I am preparing to give a talk on authentic leadership or singing "Twinkle Twinkle Little Star" for the twentieth time that day, I am connected to the vibrancy of living that I felt sitting at the cafe in Thailand. When I look in the mirror, I see a woman whose beliefs stretched and reality transformed faster than I could have imagined in that yellow-walled restaurant in Porto.

When I sat down to start writing this book, I poured over my experiences and relived each of them with fresh eyes. From scouring the stitches between the moments to spreading out the exquisite life they sewed together, I was filled with awe. It was incredible what I had done. I had transformed into warrior Kali and knocked down the pylons that held up the cathedral I no longer prayed to. In its ashes I celebrated my liberation. I cowered in fear at the emptiness that stood before me and worshiped the spaciousness. I knelt before the fullness of possibilities and exalted in my power as the alchemist of my life. I waited humbly for the spark of desire to show me what came next and then I created it. I did it again and again and again. And I will continue to do this my entire life.

Looking back, I almost couldn't believe I had navigated all these experiences over six continents. *How had I done that?* I thought about resilience, presence, trust, and all the other insights that are woven into the stories in this book. What came into focus was the totality of it all. I was ready for each moment.

We are built for reality. We have the capacity to navigate what is happening *right now*. It is real in this moment, and we are ready for it. We don't need to be equipped for the future. We don't need answers, which is just as well because we don't have them. What we have is the ability to move through each moment of life, and that's all we need.

While I was in Greece, if someone had told me that I was about to set off on a small vessel with a half-drunk captain only to be caught in a terrible storm, I would likely have stepped off the boat and waved from the dock as it sailed away. If someone told me that I was going to talk to a dead person in the temple at Burning Man, my doubts might have gotten their hooks in me and prevented the experience from happening. Thoughts of the unknowable future can capture our attention and carry us away. It is the illusion of the future and the past that often get our attention, but all that is truly real is *right now*.

In the space of this moment, there's no use for thoughts of the past or the future. Dealing with the moment is a much clearer task. Tucked inside the envelope of each moment is our inner wisdom, and it's *always* calling to us, orienting our way forward. There's nothing to do and nothing to prove. Listen for your wisdom in each moment, big and small. Draw upon the confidence that you are built for life, moment by moment, each one a raindrop falling gently from the sky. Let them each have their turn, making their little mark as they darken the ground. Let them sprinkle and splash and land as they do. Let each droplet fall and fall over years and decades until one day, a long time from now (or maybe today), you notice you have created an ocean.

MILESTONES

INNER GUIDANCE

- All that is real is this moment. We are built for reality.
- This moment is all we can navigate.
- Thoughts can spin us off into the past or the future and cause us to believe we are facing more than we are. We are only ever in one moment: *now*.
- In each moment we can call upon our intuition and access our birthright of creativity, resilience, connection, love, resourcefulness, resilience, magic, and possibility.
- Trust in your true nature. You can do this!

DEEPER NAVIGATION

1. Who do you see when you look in the mirror? How does it feel?
2. Refer to some of the insights you've reflected on in previous sections. What are your big "aha" moments?
3. With these insights, what are you inspired to do? When will you do it?
4. Be an active observer for a week. Notice how your innate abilities are always "on" and ready for you. When you feel unsure of what to say

or do, bring yourself back to this moment. What does your Voice tell you *now?* It may say to do nothing. Notice any discomfort you may feel as you slow down with this practice. Remember that you can feel discomfort and you are OK.

5. As your awareness of your ability to navigate each moment grows, you'll feel more comfortable surrendering to what life brings. Notice any ease or sense of space you feel as you embrace more of life without resistance.

CONCLUSION

I hope you have experienced some "aha" moments for yourself as you read this book. In the snap of your fingers, something extraordinary can click into place! Revel in your insights and your curiosities alike, as answers are born from questions.

But remember, this is only the beginning. When we understand something, we are often quick to say, "Okay, yeah, I get that. Great, what's next?" We don't give ourselves the space and time for what we learned to flow from our brains into our veins, for us to embody what we know in every cell of our being and live it out loud.

Invest in yourself. You are owed as much time as it takes to process the observations, curiosities, and insights that come up for you. As you chew on everything you've read, thought, and practiced here, watch how it all bubbles up in your life.

Witness what occurs as you embody all the wisdom that is innately yours. See where you are willing to apply what you've discovered and where you resist. Notice where change feels natural and where you can't seem to break a pattern. Observe how you've shifted your relationship to yourself, to others, and to the world. Tune into the changes in your relationships with loved ones and strangers. See your compassion for the driver who cuts you off in traffic or when your husband leaves dirty dishes in the sink for the zillionth time. Offer grace to yourself and others when you are stressed. Stretch how far your imagination can take you. Notice the power you wield in owning exactly who you are and honoring who you want to be. Create a powerful life and see its ripple effects in the world.

I look forward to experiencing a ripple of You.

ACKNOWLEDGMENTS

Special thank you to my dear husband Ted, my sharpest mirror and softest pillow. Without you, these adventures in my life would have never come to pass. Your support for this book was the eternal flame of inspiration I looked to in moments when I lost connection to my own. Thank you for trusting in this multi-year endeavor and for believing that what I wrote would be worth reading. *If only for you, it is enough, but I know you would say that even if only for me, it is perfect.*

To Ohm, my child, who lives both within and without me, thank you for participating in the most intimate transformation of my life. You are the magic in the stars and the tenderness in my heart. You have stretched me and grounded me, brought me life's greatest expansion, and sent me tumbling to my knees. I know you have watched over me throughout this entire process and looked on with an utmost delight as I birthed this book.

My most humble thank you to the great teachers, mentors, and gurus who showed up along my path. Ram Dass, you are the unyielding voice of compassion that speaks within me when I ask. With one small spark you lit up my entire life, and you graced me with the time to discover everything that has now been illuminated. To Jennie Harland-Khan, my coach and mentor, thank you for believing in me. Those words may number few, but they roar mightily. I know you understand.

A million thank yous to Parvati Markus, my editor and author of my Foreword, who serendipitously came into my life at the exact moment I needed you. Yes, I needed an editor, but more accurately I needed to trust the next step on my path. I was feeling the wobbles and in you came, shining light on the process of authorship. I am forever grateful for your wise, nurturing brand of magic.

APPENDIX

TRAVEL CHRONOLOGY

2017

Oct-Nov	Thailand
Dec	Laos
	Cambodia
	Vietnam
	Singapore (X-mas)

2018

Jan	New Zealand
	Australia
Feb	Mexico
Feb-Mar	Santa Monica, California
April-May	Colombia
June-Aug	Greece
Aug	Burning Man
Sept-Oct	Portugal
	Morocco
Nov	Austin, Texas
	Esalen, California
Dec	Ojai, California (X-Mas)

2019

Nov	New Mexico

ABOUT THE AUTHOR

Danielle Sunberg is a wellness entrepreneur, transformational coach, and keynote speaker. A former Big Law attorney, Danielle worked as a corporate litigator at an award-winning law firm in Washington D.C. After successfully defending her client at trial against a $6 billion judgment, Danielle left the firm to discover what truly inspired her. Along her travels, Danielle trained with some of the most preeminent mentors in conscious living and energy healing modalities, inspiring her life's work to help people claim their power—the key to living an extraordinary life. Danielle speaks internationally on authentic leadership and currently serves as a transformational coach and advisor to leaders with big life dreams. Having worked in the corporate world and as an entrepreneur whose wellness brand was acquired in 2021, Danielle understands the desires and demands of high achievers.

Danielle currently lives with her family among the live oak trees in Austin, Texas.

If this book has struck a chord with you and you'd like to follow her online, learn more about her programs, courses, and other opportunities, or contact her directly, go to www.daniellesunberg.com. Follow her on LinkedIn at www.linkedin.com/in/danielle-sunberg.

Made in the USA
Coppell, TX
10 January 2023

10801890R00114